Pr

w,

nd the

of Community

SUNY Series, Education and Culture:
Critical Factors in the Formation of
Character and Community in American Life

Eugene F. Provenzo, Jr. and Paul Farber, editors

Hurricane Andrew, The Public Schools, and the Rebuilding of Community

Eugene F. Provenzo, Jr.
and
Sandra H. Fradd

State University of New York Press

Cover photographs and collage by Marci Fiedler, Southwood Middle School Magnet Photography Program, Dade County Public Schools, Miami, Florida. Thanks to Colette Stemple, lead teacher in the program, for her help in obtaining this series of images.

Published by
State University of New York Press, Albany

For information, address the State University of New York Press,
State University Plaza, Albany, NY 12246

Production by Christine Lynch
Marketing by Theresa Abad Swierzowski

Library of Congress Cataloging-in-Publication Data

Provenzo, Eugene F.
    Hurricane Andrew, the public schools, and the rebuilding of
community / by Eugene F. Provenzo, Jr. and Sandra H. Fradd.
        p.   cm. — (SUNY series, education and culture)
    Includes bibliographical references (p.   ) and index.
        ISBN 0-7914-2481-2 (alk. paper). — ISBN 0-7914-2482-0 (pbk. :
alk. paper)
        1. Public schools—Florida—Dade County. 2. Community and school-
-Florida—Dade County. 3. Hurricane Andrew, 1922. I. Fradd,
Sandra H., 1941-   . II. Title. III. Series.
LA259.D3P76 1995
371'.01'0975938—dc20   94-28873
                                                                   CIP

10 9 8 7 6 5 4 3 2 1

CONTENTS

INTRODUCTION

Hurricane Andrew struck South Florida early on Monday morning August 24, 1992. Widely described as the worst natural disaster in modern U.S. history, the storm left thirty-eight people dead in South Florida, 80,000 homes destroyed, and damage estimated at $20 billion dollars or more. The area devastated by the hurricane was approximately three times the size of the island of Manhattan. About 250,000 people were left homeless by Andrew—a population roughly the size of the city of Las Vegas, Nevada.[1] Garbage generated by the storm in a single night was equal to the projected landfill for Dade County for the next thirty years.

This work addresses the experience of the Dade County Public Schools (DCPS)—its teachers, students, administrators, and staff during the first school year following Hurricane Andrew. In particular, it examines the role of the schools in helping people cope with a disaster of the magnitude of Hurricane Andrew and, more specifically, with the role of the schools in rebuilding community.

Relatively little research has been done concerning the impact of natural disasters on the schools and the communities they serve. Most of the research focuses on the psychological effect of disasters. Only a few studies address the experience of children: not one examines the role of the schools in reestablishing community and culture in the aftermath of a catastrophe. This work asks questions about the rebuilding process and about the efforts of administrators, teachers, counselors and parents in reestablishing normalcy after the chaos of the storm. The following are among the key questions addressed by this research: 1. How were the public schools affected by Hurricane Andrew? 2. What role did the schools play in reestablishing a sense of order and continuity in the community after the disaster? 3. How were teachers and administrators affected by the disaster, both in their work and in their personal lives?

This book was begun a few days after Hurricane Andrew struck South Florida. As a collaboration, it was undertaken by the authors as part of a highly personal, shared effort to help in the process of rebuilding the South Florida community. It is a work very much shaped by the experience of having lived through the hurricane and its aftermath. It is also a work shaped by our experience as Floridians—one of us having lived here since her childhood and the other for most of his professional life. The first pages of this manuscript were written in an unair-conditioned office at the University of Miami the week after the storm as the smell of rotting vegetation permeated the air. Off in the distance, through the open windows, one could hear the roar of chain saws cutting up fallen trees and bulldozers pushing aside debris.

Both authors experienced the storm directly: one relatively safe while taking care of an older relative on the edges of the storm in a house in Palm Beach County; and the other huddled in an interior hallway of his Coral Gables home with his wife, two cats, and a fellow professor from the university while 164 mile per hour winds roared through the neighborhood.

This work is intended both as a chronicle and an evolving sociological analysis of the teachers, students, administrators, and staff who lived through and coped with the physical and psychological consequences of the storm. Since the authors have been part of that experience, in a certain sense this work represents a participant observation study.

Specifically, both authors have had to adjust to "life after the storm": weeks without electricity and water and intersections without traffic lights. We had colleagues in desperate need of housing and help with their personal lives. We have relived over and over again, with friends and colleagues, the terrifying experience of the hurricane itself. We have experienced the frustration over the slowness of state and federal response to the hurricane. We have felt the insensitivity of many people outside South Florida to the magnitude of the storm and the feeling of abandonment as the significance of Hurricane Andrew rapidly receded from the national consciousness.[2]

The authors have also been drawn together in a closer sense of community and have admired the heroism of many of their colleagues, friends, and fellow South Floridians. They believe that the experience of the storm and its destruction has had many positive benefits along with its problems.

Hurricane Andrew, like the 1992 riots in Los Angeles, the floods in the Midwest in the summer of 1993, and the January 1994 earthquake in Northridge, California, brought South Florida its fifteen minutes of terrible attention across the United States. The reality, however, is that the problems associated with the storm will be with the community for years to come, and the experience of the storm will shape South Floridians long after the rebuilding of homes, schools, and businesses is complete.

We believe that the schools, perhaps as much as any public institution, have provided continuity and stability—as well as the possibility of new beginnings—for the South Florida community. We also believe that the teachers, administrators, and staff who work in the schools have been key to the critical role played by the schools in the rebuilding process. With this thought in mind, we dedicate this work to the teachers, administrators, and staff members of the Dade County Public Schools, and in particular to everyone who made the 1992-1993 school year possible at Pine Villa, Bowman Foster Ashe, and Gilbert Porter Elementary Schools.

On a more personal level, we would like to thank John Fradd for his excellent sense of humor and patience, and Asterie Baker Provenzo for her supportive environment and careful editing. Thanks also go to Orson, who always helped us keep our work in perspective.

NOTES

1. Sun-Sentinel, *Andrew! Savagery From the Sea, August 24, 1992* (Orlando, Florida: Tribune Publishing, 1992), p. 8.

2. Tony Proscio, "What Do We Say to Our Children?" *Miami Herald*, September 8, 1992, p. 21a. Proscio, an associate editor for *Miami Herald*, explained the fading national awareness to the crisis as follows: "In that calm hinterland known as the rest of the United States the obliteration of South Dade County is quickly becoming yesterday's news. It was bound to happen. South Florida has long suffered a semi-foreign status in the national mind, classed with exotic capitals where the folk are supposedly sturdy and accustomed to grief, places where hardship is, sorry to say, just part of a hostile and alien terrain."

1
Hurricane Andrew and South Florida: The Beginning

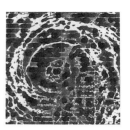

Historically, Florida has suffered the impact of hurricanes more than any other part of the country. Of the 151 major hurricanes that made landfall in the United States between 1900 and 1989, fifty-four struck Florida; Texas and Louisiana ranked second and third with thirty-six and twenty-four storms each. Four of the five most powerful storms of the century—including Andrew—hit somewhere along the Florida Coast.[1]

South Florida is the most hurricane prone region of the United States. On a scale of one to five, it ranks number one in the likelihood of suffering the impact of future storms. Despite this fact, most Floridians were unprepared for Hurricane Andrew. A major hurricane had not hit South Florida since Donna (a Category 4 storm) in 1960. In fact, the great majority of South Floridians had never experienced a hurricane.

Andrew was a Category 4 hurricane.[2] The only storm to hit Florida with stronger winds was the Category 5 hurricane that struck the Florida Keys in 1935.[3] The 1935 storm, although responsible for the death of 400 people, was less serious in that it struck a relatively unpopulated area. In the case of Hurricane Andrew, no previous storm of this size and magnitude had directly struck a major urban center, such as Dade County.

Before Hurricane Andrew, the worst storm to hit Dade County was the Category 4 hurricane that struck Miami Beach and Miami on September 18, 1926. Although both Andrew and the 1926 storm were Category 4 hurricanes, the 1926 hurricane was very different from Andrew, cutting a path of destruction from Homestead to Moore Haven on Lake Okeechobee. While the hurricane in 1926 was "huge, slow and sloppy," Andrew has been described as being "like a killer pit bull—small, strong, quick and incredibly mean."[4] Although Andrew is widely

5

recognized in financial terms as being the worst natural disaster in modern American history, it is frightening to imagine what its impact would have been if it had hit even ten or fifteen miles further north, cutting a swath across Key Biscayne, Miami Beach, and downtown Miami. Many more people would have died. Estimated financial losses could have been as high as $50 or $60 billion.

The eye of the storm came ashore in the southern half of the county. Its major impact was on suburban and rural areas away from the county's primary business and population centers. Miami Beach and downtown Miami, with their condominiums and high rise office structures, were spared the worst impact of the storm. Damage to the west coast of Florida was also minimized because the storm spent much of its fury over the southernmost area of the Everglades before reaching the west coast where it picked up strength again as it went out over the Gulf of Mexico and north towards Louisiana. (see figure 1.1)

Hurricane Andrew's eye measured between eight and ten miles across. (see figure 1.2) Maximum winds recorded from the storm were 169 miles per hour. Sustained winds over water were 150 miles per hour but were reduced to 140 miles per hour when striking land. The maximum storm surge recorded for Andrew was 16.9 feet.[5] Immediately following the storm, 1.4 million homes were left without electricity. In terms of lives lost, it was the twenty-third most deadly storm in United States history.[6]

BEFORE THE STORM

As a lazy tropical depression located to the southeast of Florida, Hurricane Andrew did not gain much attention until Saturday morning August 21, 1992. At that time, the storm was 800 miles east of Miami with winds a little over seventy-five miles per hour. By Saturday evening people were being advised to evacuate the Florida Keys. The authors were attending a faculty back-to-school picnic to welcome their new dean to the University of Miami. The picnic was being held on Key Largo in the upper Florida Keys. Just a few minutes after the dean had been given a "Hurricane" T-shirt, coffee mug, and cap to welcome him to the University of Miami (the home of the "'Canes," national football champions), the Florida Highway Patrol came through the neighborhood telling residents that a hurricane was coming and that the Keys would have to be evacuated. This was at about 5:00 P.M. The dean—a transplant from Wisconsin and not used to tropical storms—wondered out loud if the situation was really serious as people grabbed their picnic gear, loaded their cars, and headed north as quickly as possible.

A secretary in the School of Education of the University of Miami, Suzanne Schorle, who was attending the picnic, mentioned to one of the authors that her children were scheduled to return the following Monday from Pennsylvania where they were visiting their grandparents. Monday, of course, was the day that the hurricane struck. The children never returned to South Florida. Their home was demolished, and Schorle and her husband were permanently displaced by the storm. The husband's job, which involved a small computer related business, was destroyed because of the hurricane, and he moved back to Pennsylvania to join his children. Schorle stayed on until early November to settle insurance matters and sell the family's house, and then she, too, moved to Pennsylvania.

Schorle's experience was similar to that of thousands of others throughout the county. By the beginning of November 1992, it was estimated that approximately 90,000 people would move as a result of the storm—over half of them permanently out of Dade and Broward counties.[7]

Other than the initial evacuation from the Keys and trips out for basic supplies, not much was accomplished by most people as Saturday evening passed. Most people were still unsure what to do or to expect as they watched the weather reports on their television sets and wondered whether or not this was really going to be "the Big One" that had been predicted for years. South Florida was being warned that all preparations had to be made by nightfall on Sunday.

By Sunday morning it was clear that the storm was on a direct collision course with South Florida. People battened down their houses and made runs for whatever supplies they could find in crowded supermarkets and hardware stores. By the afternoon most hardware stores and lumber yards were empty of any useful items. A sense of panic grew as grocery stores were emptied of all bottled water, canned goods, and paper products. Well into Sunday evening many people continued to prepare for the storm. One of the authors, Gene Provenzo, was still bolting storm shutters onto the windows of his house at 10:00 P.M., as the storm rapidly approached on a direct collision course with South Florida.

FIGURE 1.1. The Track of Hurricane Andrew August 16-28, 1993

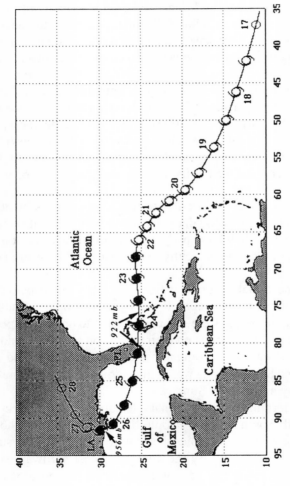

Best track positions for Hurricane Andrew (August 16-28, 1992). Positions at 00 and 12 UTC are shown. Dates are at the 00 UTC locations. Tropical depression, tropical storm and hurricane strengths are represented by open circles and open and filled hurricane symbols, respectively. Locations of lowest minimum central pressure are shown. Data for this and other black and white figures are from National Hurricane Center's preliminary report.

Source: National Hurricane Center, National Oceanic and Atmospheric Administration.

FIGURE 1.2. Hurricane Andrew Over South Florida

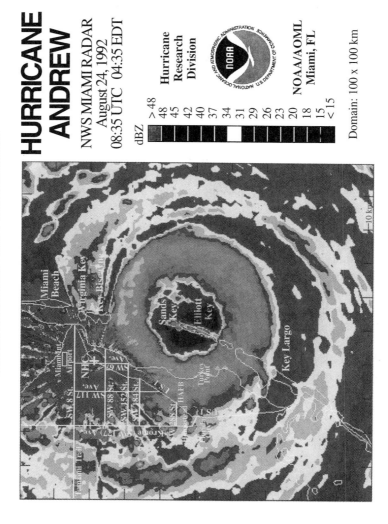

**HURRICANE
ANDREW**

NWS MIAMI RADAR
August 24, 1992
08:35 UTC 04:35 EDT

dBZ
> 48
48
45
42
40
37
34
31
29
26
23
20
18
15
< 15

Hurricane
Research
Division

NOAA/AOML
Miami, FL

Domain: 100 x 100 km

Source: National Hurricane Center, National Oceanic and Atmospheric Administration.

Prior to the storm, the school system played an important leadership role in preparing the community for the storm and in promoting individual household preparations. The majority of the county's Red Cross shelters were located in schools. The school system provided information on the availability of the shelters and offered suggestions on the types of supplies that people needed to take with them to the shelters. In addition, the school district broadcast information about the storm and how to prepare for it in English, Spanish, and Haitian Creole, the three major languages of the Greater Miami Area. The Dade County Public School System owns both its own radio station, WLRN, and television station, WLRN, channel 17. According to Maria Santamaria, Community Relations Specialist for Spanish Language Information, Dade County Public Schools, the school system also provided other radio and television stations with storm information in multiple languages through its community public relations office. These same services were used after the storm to tell people where to go for assistance, to inform them of the opening of stores and emergency aid facilities, and to promote the initial steps in the rebuilding process. For newly arrived immigrants, unfamiliar with the language and culture of the community, public information in their own language was an important component of the disaster preparedness and recovery process.[8]

Throughout most of Sunday morning and afternoon, traffic was jammed on all of the major arteries leading north of Miami for 120 miles. Sandra Fradd found herself caught in one of the largest traffic jams in history as many people fled South Florida for safer regions to the north. It took her three and one-half hours to make what would normally have been a forty-five minute trip to Boca Raton.

IN THE EYE OF THE STORM

As the storm approached, most people tracked its progress on the local television stations. Bryan Norcross, a meteorologist with Channel 4, became an immediate celebrity as he described the approaching storm and advised people how to prepare for and survive it.[9]

On Sunday morning before the storm, pleas were made by county officials for all available medical personnel to volunteer their services at the local evacuation centers. All women in their final term of pregnancy were requested to go to Jackson Memorial Hospital where a special medical support team had been assembled. By 10:00 P.M. Sunday evening the halls of Jackson Memorial Hospital were lined with more than 400 pregnant women.

By Sunday evening 180,000 people had been evacuated to emergency shelters out of low-lying flood zones. Most of these shelters were schools. At almost the last moment possible, emergency management officials realized that many homeless people, living in cardboard shelters under the freeway in downtown Miami, had not been evacuated. Four buses were sent out to take them to local shelters. By 10:00 P.M. bus service was terminated and by 10:30 P.M. police were telling everyone to get off the streets.

At 11:00 P.M. heavy winds and rains were being reported from Fort Lauderdale to southern Dade County. By midnight, the television reporter, Bryan Norcross, described the storm as "beginning to rock-and-roll." At this time, the National Hurricane Center said that the thrust of the hurricane would be felt for the next twelve to sixteen hours. At midnight Sunday Norcross brought the immediacy of the storm home to South Floridians by simply telling them that "absolutely, there is no doubt about it, it is going to happen tonight."

Brilliant bursts of blue-green tinged lightning lit the sky as the winds began to increase to over one-hundred miles per hour. By 2:00 A.M., trees were overturning and blocking roads all over the county. People throughout the county began to lose power at about this time. The eyewall of the storm entered Biscayne Bay at 4:28 A.M., Monday, August 24, 1992. At that time all police and fire personnel were ordered off the streets. A few minutes later in Coral Gables, the storm blew the National Hurricane Center's radar system off the roof. At 5:20 A.M. the wind gauge at the Hurricane Center recorded a speed of 164 miles per hour and then broke.[10]

People were advised by television and radio announcers to get away from any exterior walls or windows, to get to a central room—even a closet—and to have mattresses available to put over them. As windows shattered and roofs were torn off, people began to wonder when the storm would finally end. Karen Baldwin, an elementary school teacher living in the area just north of the eye of the hurricane, described how at the height of the storm, she, her husband Scott, and their teenage son Doug barricaded themselves in a closet in a protected bedroom. Her description of what then happened was similar to that of many individuals who were in the main path of the storm:

The wind was so loud that you could not talk or hear without shouting. . . .
The noise level got to be eerie. To me, it was absolutely the most horrible
noise that you could imagine. Everybody says it sounds like a freight train.
It was much worse than a freight train, between the howling and the
whistling of the wind. It was an incredible, indescribable noise. . . . I
grabbed Doug's Walkman, put the headphones on and turned the volume
up full blast, which in effect did drown out a good portion of the noise. It
didn't drown it all out, but it made it that much more bearable because I
was listening to a very calm voice on the radio talking people through the
storm—the voice of Bryan Norcross.

We could hear the screen patio tearing away from the back of the house. We
could actually hear the metal bending and ripping. . . . Attempting to open
or closing any interior door after 4:00 o'clock in the morning was incredibly
difficult to do. . . . Probably the height of the storm hit us at five o'clock. I
was scared. I've never been so scared in my life. I realized I was sitting in
the room shaking. At least I thought I was shaking. And then I kind of
took a deep breath and realized that it wasn't me shaking, it was the wall
behind me that was literally moving back and forth, almost vibrating. At
that point, someone on the radio said if you don't feel secure where you are,
you might want to seek an interior hallway in the house with no windows.
So, I announced this to Doug and Scott. . . . We no sooner got the door
open, and the wind literally threw Scott across the room. As we went out,
the living room door blew, at which point all three of the French doors in
the back of the house broke. We literally crawled back to the bedroom,
got the door closed again pushed the dresser back up to door and were
frantically trying to close the outside French doors into the bedroom. They
had blown out and we were holding onto the doors trying to hold them
closed. It was impossible. Between the three of us we could not get them
closed. The storm continued . . . I opened the bedroom door to check on the
front doors. This was probably the height of stupidity for the evening. The
whole force of the storm was coming through our front doors. I decided I
had to close the front doors. So I went over to the doors and I tried to get the
one door closed and I got it two thirds closed. And I had to reach over to get
the other door. So I am standing kind of almost spread eagle in the doorway.
And, of course, all this wind and rain and everything else was coming
through the doors. It was as if I was flying between the wind and the
water. . . . The wind just took me and literally pushed me backwards toward
the wall in the dining room. It probably just pushed me about ten feet. . . . It
was very surreal, the whole thing was surreal. I could see the doors, the
wind and the water coming in. And there I was just slowly moving backwards with the force of the wind and the water.[11]

Retreating back to the bedroom and an interior closet with her husband and son, Karen rode out the rest of the storm and waited to see just how bad the damage was to their home. A home that had been a haven, a safe place of retreat from the worries and cares of an outside life was no longer secure, breached by the extraordinary violence of the hurricane. (Baldwin Interview)

Faye McCloud, a counselor at Bowman Foster Ashe Elementary School, recalled her experience with the hurricane as being "horrendous." As she explained:

> I had never been in a hurricane. . . . I was very ill-prepared for the hurricane—for what happened. I have two children, a three year old and a five year old. At the time of the hurricane, they were two and four. It has just been horrendous. I'm still consumed by the effects of the storm. It's just not ending.[12]

McCloud and her family lived a mile east of Metrozoo on 157th Street. The storm totally destroyed their house. Initially, like many other Miamians, she underestimated the potential destructiveness of the storm:

> I had popped pop corn. We had candles. I thought that we were going to be in the house and be cozy. Twenty minutes into the main part of the hurricane, the window in my daughter's room blew. I had just taken the kids from their room and put them in our room. That was about 4:45 A.M. (McCloud Interview)

In retrospect, there is an almost mundane and seemingly casual quality to McCloud's approach to the storm. As she explained:

> I had woken up about 1:30 A.M. and cleaned up and vacuumed. We had a new aqua carpet and I wanted to be prepared in case the electricity went off. About 4:30 my husband told me to look out of the window. I looked out and I was very frightened. I had never seen trees bend over like I saw them doing. I remember I told him that I was nervous. The sky had such an odd color and there was such tension around us, as if we knew that something was about to happen. We lit the candles. My husband was attempting to put something over the windows when they blew. I grabbed the kids and ran to the garage that was attached to the house and put the kids in the car. My husband said: "Faye, I have to go back in and blow out the candles." I said: "No, you can't go back in there. The hurricane is in the house." He said: "I need to go in and get the keys so we can move the car closer to the wall so the kitchen door won't bang open." I begged him not to go. Then he said: "I need to check on our neighbor who is by herself. "I told him:

"You cannot go! You cannot go! You just have to stay here!!" Then we got in the second car that didn't have as much glass as the first. (McCLoud Interview)

Like many people describing the hurricane at its worst, McCloud recalled:

the horrible sound overhead—like a train. But as much as I was afraid, I didn't want to display that to the children. So we sang songs and named all of the people that we could think of that we know and said: "They're thinking of us." . . . we were so hot. . . . We just stayed there hearing all of the horrible sounds of things hitting the garage, not knowing what it was. We were terrified. We were afraid that the garage door would break open. (McCloud Interview)

Once the storm was over, McCloud's husband went inside their house:

When he came back, he was crying. He said: "Faye, I just can't believe it. Our house is gone." I could not even believe what he was telling me. I couldn't comprehend what he was saying. So I went inside and he stayed in the car with the kids. I could not believe it. It was just beyond anything that you might see in a theater—in a good movie where you feel that you are there. Except, I was really there. I was so stunned, and so shocked, and so hurt. (McCloud Interview)

AFTER THE STORM

After the storm people across the county emerged from their houses to face massive devastation and destruction. Where he lives in Coral Gable, Gene Provenzo found virtually all of the huge ficus trees in his neighborhood uprooted and laying across lawns, streets, and even houses. In describing the scene to family and friends up north, it was impossible to communicate how the tropical ficus trees, with their extraordinarily dense vegetation and thick and twining root systems and branches, blocked, not just the roadways, but even the light and the breeze. No one could walk more than a couple of hundred feet beyond their houses without being blocked by mounds of what would be, in a couple of days, rotting vegetation. Cars could not pass through the neighborhood for several days and even then had to be driven across previously carefully manicured lawns. Driving became even more of a challenge at major traffic intersections where missing stoplights would not be replaced for weeks to come. In most cases, drivers were careful and tried to avoid creating problems by yielding the right-of-way and giving signals to each other as they proceeded through intersections and traffic areas.

A surreal quality was evident everywhere following the hurricane. There were no leaves on the trees. It was as though a winter frost had appeared and killed everything in sight. At the same time, houses were covered with a green haze of plant vegetation. For several days, the air was extraordinarily clear. There was no dust. It had literally been blown away by the storm. Without the shade from the trees, without the diffusion of the sun's heat by dust in the air, sunny South Florida became hot and harsh. People accustomed to air-conditioning suffered. Coral Gables was a community considered to have come through the hurricane relatively well. The really major destruction began three to five miles further south where people emerging from their houses were apt to describe what they saw as "looking like a bomb had dropped," "like Hiroshima," or like a "war zone."

One of the authors, Sandra Fradd, who was staying with her mother in Boca Raton, watched with millions of others as the first images of the destruction were telecast from South Florida. Initially, the news shots of the downtown Miami area made it appear that the storm was nothing more than a nuisance. However, as the news reporters went up in their helicopters and began to fly south, it became clear that the damage was extraordinary and widespread. What struck her most was the dazed looks and disorientation that so profoundly marked the faces of the people whose images were captured on the television that Monday morning. The level of destruction in whole neighborhoods where she had recently traveled and worked was hard to comprehend. It soon became evident that much of South Florida was totally cut off from the rest of the world.

For the survivors of the storm in the southern part of the county, the news helicopters could transmit the images of what had happened but were unable to meet any of the needs of the survivors who had lost so much. The television images of the destruction were immediately sent out worldwide. Everywhere people were moved by the sight of the massive destruction and suffering. Homestead Air Force base was literally flattened. Reporters on local television stations commented over and over again that they had no idea while the storm was going on that it could have caused the sort of destruction that had taken place. A reporter flying in an open helicopter described how he saw "numerous homes down to the ground. I did not see any homes—not one home south of Kendall Drive without damage—extensive damage. . . . I've never seen a nuclear attack before but that's what I would envision happening."[13]

People remarked that for once the images and the messages conveyed by television could not accurately portray the severity of the disaster. Howard Kleinberg, in his account of the first days of the hurricane, noted the differences between the impact of the storm portrayed by the media and the harshness of the reality of the disaster:

> When phone lines finally opened and friends and relatives from around the country called to see how we were, my wife Natalie told them that whatever they saw on television was mild compared to how it actually was. After many years of people claiming television hyped and exaggerated events, Miamians were now saying that nothing seen on the tube adequately could portray what occurred on the morning of August 24, 1992.[14]

Weeks would pass before anything even beginning to approach normalcy returned.

People coming out of the storm expressed a sense of shock and disbelief. Many wondered if others were as badly "hit" as they were. Some people in the areas of greatest destruction in South County initially thought that the reason they had received no help or assistance was that the more northern and central parts of Dade County must have been damaged even more severely than they were. They imagined that they were among the few survivors in the area, that it must have been even worse elsewhere. This was the only possible explanation they could come up with to explain the lack of assistance.

Cut off as they were from all aspects of life as they had known it just twelve hours earlier, these disoriented and storm struck people began to devise their own ways of surviving. For many, cars and trucks, as well as their homes, had been totally destroyed. Roads were impassable, even when a vehicle still functioned.

With only a few of their possessions intact, survivors in the most severely struck areas banded together to share their meager resources. They were faced with a reality most of them had never thought possible. For the majority, their homes no longer had roofs, their possessions had been scattered by the wind and soaked by the rain, and they were totally cut off from communication with the outside world.

As personal reports began to come out of the south end of the county, people told reporters and others about terrifying hours spent with three and four people huddled in a small closet or bathroom. Stories of people surviving in bathtubs with mattresses drawn over the top of their heads as the roof peeled off above them became commonplace. A new way of greeting people pervaded the community and continued for several months after the storm. How did you do? and Where were you during the storm? became the first questions people asked each other when they met.

Six hundred thousand people, or seventy-two percent of Dade County, were left without power immediately after the storm. The area south of Kendall Avenue was declared a restricted zone, and no one was allowed in unless they lived in the area or had a special reason for being there. Roofs were caved in everywhere south of Kendall. Buses were blown over on their sides. Large boats were stranded in backyards hundreds of feet from the water. Medical services were stretched to the maximum. In the emergency rooms of hospitals across the county people arrived with severe cuts and wounds.

Tragedies and extraordinary stories of survival emerged in the days and weeks following the storm. There were tales of people being decapitated in front of loved ones by flying glass and beams. There were accounts of pets being swept away in the wind. Stories of people moving out of rooms just before roofs were blown away or walls collapsed were told again and again. Children described "camping in the closet" and seeing their houses "break."

Looting began almost immediately after the storm in many neighborhoods. Preventing looting became a matter of personal survival and a constant source of tension and fear. Although the police and the National Guard were present throughout the county, they were at first too few in number to provide necessary protection. Many neighborhoods set up local patrols who checked on anyone who was not familiar. Fear permeated the neighborhoods—fear not only of being robbed or attacked by looters but also of being mistaken for a looter as one searched for friends and loved ones.

Traffic jams caused by people trying to return to their homes from shelters made getting around almost impossible for several days. On Thursday August 25, 1992, three days after the storm, one of the authors made his way from his own neighborhood to some of the worst hit areas in the county. He was able to do so as part of the relief effort, driven by his new next-door neighbor, Deborah Stone, who had moved into her in-laws' home with her husband and two children after the hurricane had destroyed her family's house and possessions in the Mediterranean I complex, just north of Perrine.

Mediterranean I is in the neighborhood of Country Walk—one of the worst hit housing developments in the hurricane's path. Roads were barely passible. American flags flew from the top of what remained of roofs or were draped over the front of battered houses and on crudely constructed flag poles. Signs asking for help from insurance companies such as Prudential, Allstate and State Farm were spray painted on walls identifying families and insurance policy numbers. Defiance and survival were reflected in the messages that accompanied the requests for assistance. "Andrew Sucks," "Life begins at 165 mph!" "Andy's Come But We are Not," "In a Few Months He'll be Forgotten," "Screw You, Andrew!", and "Wipe Your Feet," demonstrated that people still had a sense of humor while "Looters will be shot Dead," "Looters will be shot—no questions asked," and "Never alone—you loot—we shoot," reflected the very real threat of robbery and violence that people were beginning to experience in the devastated neighborhoods.

Survivors in the Mediterranean I development described how they spent the night guarding their homes and chasing off looters who were driving through their neighborhood with the lights on their cars turned off looking for houses that were unprotected and open. Driving around a corner to leave a note on a friend's house, Gene Provenzo and Deborah Stone were confronted by a middle-aged man with a hunting knife strapped to his leg and a pistol in a holster at his side. He wanted to know what they were doing in the neighborhood and communicated very clearly that they were not welcome.

Many people lost everything that they owned. Among colleagues in our department at the university, approximately half sustained damage so severe that they had to move out of their homes or, at the very least, had to undergo major reconstruction involving new roofs and complete interior renovations. Hurricane Andrew was an event that would be relived in casual conversations, in bad dreams, and in stray memories for a long time to come.

THE FEDERAL RESPONSE TO THE STORM

Little or no coordination of relief efforts took place during the first seventy-two hours following the storm. Many problems stemmed from the magnitude of the catastrophe, but others were clearly a result of a lack of communication within the local government and the failure of the federal government to efficiently send military resources into the area. Both government officials and residents alike had failed to anticipate and prepare for the possible damage of a hurricane like Andrew. As a result, the first attempts to provide aid to citizens who clearly needed help were feeble, inept, and, in many of the hardest hit areas, virtually nonexistent. Near the Country Walk housing development, the sign on a house with an American flag flying from its roof echoed many survivors frustration: "Andrew's Dead—We're Alive—Forget the FEDS and RED X WE WILL SURVIVE."

CONCLUSION

Hurricane Andrew was a transforming experience for many of the people in the South Florida community—something that would redefine their lives forever. It was also an experience which would redefine the social and cultural institutions of the area as well. In order to understand how the transformation occurred, it is important to understand the forces that were at work. One of the most profound effects of the storm for many people was the loss of personal control and an increased sense of vulnerability. A second effect was the lack of connectedness and isolation that many people felt in the first few days after the storm. Finally, many people who were normally independent and autonomous in their day-to-day lives found themselves dependent on others for aid and assistance in ways that they had never experienced before.

Compared to those of the 1926 hurricane, the experiences people went through as part of Andrew had some clear similarities and differences. According to the account of the 1926 hurricane by L. F. Reardon, as was the case with Hurricane Andrew, people banded together after the storm to help each other out and to share whatever meager resources they had. Patriotism and love of country also emerged as themes after both hurricanes as people flew flags as a symbol of unity and their having survived. This was particularly the case after Andrew, where house after house in the storm struck neighborhoods displayed American flags amidst the devastation and destruction.

In Reardon's account, while Marines from Key West and the National Guard patrolled in order to prevent looting, there was no major theft nor significant violence involving one group of people against another. In 1926, the world and Miami was smaller and more unified while, ironically, less informed and interconnected. In 1926, there were no helicopters flying overhead and reporting the news to the outside world immediately after the storm—no reporters making broadcasts as to the level and types of destruction that had been experienced.[15]

In 1926, people were more isolated. There was no way, for example, for anyone to know the fate of Miami Beach after the storm since the causeway had been destroyed and boats could not make their way across the bay for several days.

In 1926, there were no convenience stores, air-conditioning was not yet in use, and there was no television or radio. The community was more isolated, yet more self-reliant. In 1992, the community was much larger, more connected through radio and television, and yet, therefore, even more isolated and troubled. After Hurricane Andrew, when the fences came down and the trees were uprooted, many people were faced with having to communicate on a personal level with neighbors they often barely knew and in ways that were new to them.

Many survivors of the hurricane of 1992 shared a natural feeling of euphoria. At the same time there was the challenge posed by having to rebuild and to deal with neighbors and colleagues in ways that were new and unique.

Many Miami suburbs, imbued with anonymity, were suddenly reduced to villages and local communities. Where prior to the hurricane people largely left their neighborhoods each day to go to work, lived in their isolated homes, and knew or cared little about their neighbors, after Hurricane Andrew they were inevitably drawn together. The comforts and security provided by electricity—air-conditioning, cable television, heat for cooking, and power to activate burglar alarms—was gone. People had no choice but to venture out and deal with their community in ways that they had never previously considered.

In the following pages, we look at the role of the schools in dealing with the transformation and change created by Hurricane Andrew. We examine the role that the schools played in reestablishing a sense of continuity in the South Florida community. We believe that with Hurricane Andrew, the role of the schools in recovering from the storm was somehow more important—somehow different—than sixty-six years earlier after the 1926 hurricane. *How* and *why* is ultimately the subject of this book.

NOTES

1. Curtis Morgan and Stephen K. Doig, "Could It Happen Again?" *Miami Herald*, September 5, 1992, p. 7E.

2. A Category 4 hurricane is one in which the barometric pressure is between 27.17 to 27.90 inches with winds of 131 to 155 miles per hour and a storm surge of thirteen to eighteen feet. Damage in this category of storm is "extreme" and typically includes the almost total destruction of doors and windows. See "Measuring a Hurricane's Strength," *Miami Herald*, August 28, 1992, p. 3E.

3. Hurricanes were not given names prior to 1950.

4. Arva Moore Parks, "Until Last Week, Storm of '26 Was *The* Hurricane," August 30, 1992, *The Miami Herald*, p. 1L.

5. *Sun-Sentinel, Andrew! Savagery From the Sea, August 24, 1992* (Orlando, Florida: Tribune Publishing, 1992), 15.

6. Ibid, p. 5.

7. David Satterfield, "Pulling Up Stakes: Thousands Planning to Relocate Because of Andrew," *Miami Herald*, November 10, 1992, pp. 1A.

8. Interview with Maria Santa Maria conducted by Sandra Fradd and Eugene F. Provenzo, Jr., February 8, 1993, Miami, Florida.

9. The following section is drawn in large part from the television documentary, "Hurricane Andrew: As it Happened," produced by WTVJ-Miami, Channel 4. This documentary was developed primarily from news reports made by Channel 4 before, during, and after the storm and was distributed through the community a few months after the storm.

10. John Dorschner, "The Hurricane That Changed Everything," *Miami Herald*, August 30, 1992, p. 30A.

11. Interview with Karen Baldwin conducted by Eugene F. Provenzo, Jr., Miami, Florida, September 1, 1992. The quote that follows is from this interview and cited in the text.

12. Interview conducted by Sandra Fradd and Eugene F. Provenzo, Jr. with Faye McCloud, February 26, 1993, Miami, Florida. The quotes that follow are from this interview and are cited.

13. *Hurricane Andrew*, WTVJ-4 documentary, from news reports broadcast August 24, 1992.

14. Howard Kleinberg, *The Florida Hurricane and Disaster, 1992* (Miami: Centennial Press, 1992), p. 2.

15. L. F. Reardon, *The Florida Hurricane and Disaster* (Miami: Centennial Press, 1992), p. 16.

2

Emergency Plans of the School System and Its Initial Response

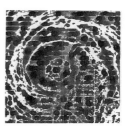

The Dade County Public School system, like most school systems across the country, has a rhythm, a set of rituals for starting each new school year.[1] Classes normally begin the day after Labor Day. The week before the opening of schools for the academic year, teachers return to set up their classrooms, to hold meetings with their colleagues, and to plan the activities for the new year. New teachers meet with the superintendent for a district and union orientation meeting. For the 1992-93 school year, however, few of these rituals were carried out. The traditional school schedule was totally disrupted by the hurricane. Not only were many schools severely damaged, but also the lives of teachers, administrators, and support staff were significantly disrupted as a result of the storm.

Early on in the recovery process, the school system came forward to provide leadership, just as they had provided shelter during the storm. In a television and radio broadcast to the community the Friday after the hurricane struck, Janet MacAllily, the chairperson of the school board, made clear how the school system was responding to the crisis. As she explained:

> For those of us who have a lesser degree of trauma in our lives, we are certainly going to make your lives as easy as possible relative to the schools, our employees and so forth . . . Mr. Visiedo [the superintendent] I think has been working in a heroic capacity to try to pull us together, and I know I speak for the school board members to say how grateful we are for such effective leadership. . . . He has of course been working on getting the schools repaired as quickly as possible so that they will be operational, so that we can open the schools as soon as is feasible.[2]

Immediate actions from the superintendent's office following the storm included establishing a shelter for school system employees who had lost their homes, making sure that people were paid despite the delay in the beginning of the school year, and providing child care for staff and employees who had special needs resulting from the storm.

The members of the board offered their personal assistance to the community in the recovery process. As part of the special broadcast following the storm, Betsy Kaplan, the vice-chair of the board, for example, talked about living at the edge of the storm zone and knowing many of the people in the affected neighborhoods. She gave her home number as part of the broadcast and requested anyone in the community to call her if she could be of assistance. William Turner talked about working in Carol City High School, helping in efforts to get people fed in the south part of the county. Rosa Castro Feinberg thanked the superintendent, the cafeteria workers, the principals and assistant principals, the teachers, and other school employees for their efforts. She briefly summarized priorities such as protecting the school structures, getting the schools ready for the children, and continuing to serve the community.

THE SCHOOLS AS SHELTERS
FOR THE COMMUNITY

Perhaps the most important function that the public schools provided both during the evacuation period, as well as during and immediately after the hurricane, was to shelter members of the community. Of the twenty-seven Red Cross shelters in operation as of September 8, 1992, twenty-six were in public schools. Forty-eight shelters were filled at the height of the storm. Crowded, often chaotic and confusing, the shelters provided a haven for people from the evacuation areas during the storm, as well as shelter after the hurricane for those who were particularly hit hard.[3]

Hialeah-Miami Lakes Senior High School, for example, provided shelter for approximately 3,000 persons during the hurricane. After a little more than a week, this number was reduced to 300 persons. In those schools out of the main impact zone of the hurricane, the availability of power made it possible in the days following the storm to provide people in the shelters with hot meals, air-conditioning, running water, and hot showers.[4]

The Red Cross shelters located in the schools—while absolutely essential for the community—created their own unique problems for the school system's recovery effort. The shelters continued to occupy valuable space after the school system began to rebuild and prepare to open after the hurricane was over. Many principals found their authority superseded by local Red Cross officials just as they were in the process of trying to get their schools up and running for the new school year. As Associate Superintendent Nelson Diaz explained, the Red Cross administrators came into many schools and told the principal:

> "You're no longer the principal. I'm the boss." They do that with other institutions, not just schools, when they utilize them as shelters. They broke down our doors in some of our sites to set up shop. It is part of an emergency management agreement in place for disasters, and the school district has these agreements in place with the Red Cross. Given the response, I don't think that any one was ever prepared for a hurricane. The Red Cross went to schools that had been identified as shelters. They did not go into just any schools. Some principals only allowed them into certain parts of the school and made it clear that was all that they got. Others gave them the whole school. Some schools were just so crowded that it was almost impossible for several days after the storm. There was a breakdown in the distribution of medical supplies to the shelters. They didn't show up in several cases. There was a sense, in some cases, that these people came in like bulldozers taking over in a emergency.[5]

For Diaz, the point was that "whether it was the military or the Red Cross, we are the ones that are running the schools. This has to be understood." (Diaz Interview)

The idea of the school system needing to remain in control of its own resources and buildings was strongly emphasized by Superintendent Visiedo who explained that the Red Cross proved somewhat more difficult to work with in the schools than the military. According to him, this was because:

> they didn't have the organized, centralized system that the military had. . . . They didn't know who was in charge. They'd go to the county when they wanted something, or they would talk to the commissioners or a state legislator.[7]

Actually, at first, the military often superseded its authority, not knowing what it should do or whom it should report to as part of emergency efforts. As Visiedo recalled, one night right after the storm, he was called at home:

The military had just kicked the doors in on a school and taken over the school—just shortly after they had arrived. They had been told by one of the county commissioners that they could just go and take over a school. The military didn't realize that the school board is independent. When I got that message, I went down and I insisted on talking with a general. I met him that night and I made it clear to him that nobody takes over any schools unless I am aware of it. He was very cooperative, understanding, and appreciative now he knew who to contact. (Visiedo Interview)

For Visiedo and the schools, the Red Cross proved a serious problem. As he explained:

The Red Cross was a real problem. They meant well, worked hard, but were very disorganized. We did everything we could to help them. In many cases, we took all the heat and did everything for them—very, very disorganized. Some of our public information problems were caused by them, not out of meanness or spite, but because they didn't know the answer. They didn't know how to deal with the whole situation of shelters. (Visiedo Interview)

Volunteer shelter administrators frequently did not know how to manage the facilities. Decisions, often made on the spur of the moment, in retrospect proved more disruptive than they would have been if a trained administrator had been in charge. At Pine Villa Elementary School, for example, teachers had spent the days immediately following the hurricane cleaning up and sorting expensive Montessori materials, which they had left out on classroom tables to dry. When Red Cross shelter volunteers arrived, the materials were swept into plastic bags and tossed aside as garbage so that the tables could be used elsewhere in the building.

This incident and similar types of problems led Visiedo and his staff to consider changes in how the school shelter programs would work in the future:

Our arrangement with the Red Cross this year will probably change to make the shelter person the principal and then have whomever they bring in as our assistant. What you have is some people who worked in banks and small operations all of a sudden found themselves in charge of this huge unit, and they thought that they were commandeering the thing. They didn't know the first thing about how to do it. We spent our time cleaning up after them and trying to eliminate problems. Our principals know how to deal with law enforcement, municipalities, bureaucracy, and everything else. One of the results that is going to come out of this is that—we are negotiating with the Red Cross right now—we are going to be in charge of the shelters. We're going to have them assist us. They will be under our command and our direction because the other way is an absolute mess. (Visiedo Interview)

PROVIDING SHELTER FOR
SCHOOL SYSTEM EMPLOYEES

While the school system provided shelters for the community, both during and after the storm, it also tried to provide help to its teachers, administrators, and staff. Estimates the week after the storm indicated that 5,000 of the school system's workers had lost their homes in the hurricane. Most found shelter with friends or relatives or were able to relocate themselves to new housing in other parts of the county.[7]

In order to help those who were unable to find a place to stay elsewhere in the community, the school system set up a temporary shelter for school system employees and their families at Ruben Dario Middle School. Ruben Dario was centrally located and had been only slightly damaged by the hurricane. Located well inland in the south central part of the county, the school is a massive structure, consisting of dozens of classrooms, a large cafeteria, and an auditorium.

More than just shelter was provided by the school system. In addition to providing school systems employees with a place to stay in the first days after the storm, the program set up at Ruben Dario also helped school system families with assistance in finding housing, provided free clothing and hot meals, and also psychological counseling.

On a long-term basis, housing was also provided by the school system to its employees at the hotel facility that was part of the vocational program at Lindsey Hopkins Technical Education Center. These services proved to be needed on a long-term basis by only a few people.

THE SUPERINTENDENT SETS IN MOTION
THE RECOVERY EFFORT

Immediately following the storm, the federal government, relief agencies such as the Red Cross, and local county officials were criticized for inadequately responding to the crisis. On August 27, three days after the storm, Kate Hale, the Dade County Emergency Director, asked on national television, with tears welling in her eyes, "Where the hell is the cavalry on this one?" Later the same day President Bush finally deployed 30,000 troops to the south Dade area to help with relief efforts.

Of the local organizations responding to the crisis, probably none was more effective than the school system. Why was this the case? To begin with, the school system is centralized and countywide and not affected by the divisions imposed as a result of local municipalities. Resources from the north end of the county, which was largely unaffected in terms of the immediate storm, could be drawn upon to cope with the crisis in the south. In addition, the school system was under the command of a single individual—Superintendent Visiedo.[8]

Visiedo, with the support of the school board, responded quickly and effectively to the poststorm crisis. This response was in marked contrast to those of politicians such as Dade County Mayor Steve Clark, who did nothing after the storm; the mayor remained holed up in his house in the north part of the county, insisting that directing the relief effort was not his job.[9] In contrast, efforts on the part of the school system to begin rebuilding began immediately after the storm. On Monday morning, Visiedo assembled an executive management team and supporting subteams to begin assessing damage. Principals were asked to assess the needs of their schools as quickly as possible. With the cooperation of the school board and the Florida Department of Education, key statutory provisions were waived so that reroofing of damaged schools could begin as soon as two days after the storm.

Immediately following the storm, Visiedo's main concern was about the condition of the hundreds of portable classrooms located throughout the county. As he explained:

> They aren't the most stable things. As it turned out, the portables fared better than the buildings in some cases. Our construction code was very solid. I remember going to Campbell Drive Elementary and the middle school which are right next to each other and had sustained substantial damage. Our portables were intact right there and they faced 160 mile an hour winds. When I realized that the portables were in pretty good shape, the biggest concern was assessing the damage inside the buildings, and assessing the damage districtwide. I didn't realize that . . . every school had been damaged to some degree . . . I didn't realize the extent that the damage had increased the further south you went. When I started visiting those

schools, and walked into schools like Southwood, Pine Villa, Mays, Homestead Senior, I was really taken aback to see the destruction that had taken place there.[10]

Visiedo was out inspecting schools by the evening after the storm:

I couldn't get to many of the schools because everything was so slow. I got stopped everywhere. They let me through because I was the superintendent. We got as far as Campbell Drive on that first day. And then every day after that. I never came into the office. I was out on the road. If I had to have meetings, I had them in the schools until we started making formal debriefing plans. We were meeting at MIS [Management Information Systems] which is further south and west, and readily accessible by the turnpike. I moved my operation to the affected area. We had to meet every day. We started in the morning with a debriefing, got information, damage reports, the issues. Every day we had a different set of problems that emerged, like assessing the FP&L [Florida Power and Light] schedule for the schools that were out. It was an incredible logistical process. (Visiedo Interview)

For Visiedo, one of the most of the most serious difficulties in implementing the recovery had to do with the constant problem of rumors:

Rumors would begin out of nowhere. Literally, within a matter of hours, you had a crisis on your hands because the word had spread throughout the community that something was going to happen. Things that I hadn't even thought of yet could happen. For example, at Southwood, there was a processing center and military station down there. The Red Cross was there. All of a sudden there was a rumor that we were planning on throwing them out the next day. I started receiving phone calls from citizens and the military, the media, asking how we were going to do this. I have no idea how it started. . . . We had to fashion our messages in such a way that we were going to kill rumors by dealing with them. That was extremely time-consuming. When you looked at the scope of things that you had to do, I found it offensive that I would have to spend that much time on media and communication. But I found that it was a necessity. I think that my energies could have been better used in other places. But as it worked out that was a critical and very important part of the process. (Visiedo Interview)

Many of the school system people made extraordinary efforts—despite often having lost their own homes. As Visiedo explained:

I couldn't have been prouder of the way that the people set aside their own personal things to help. Everybody on my executive management

team had personal problems— some people totally lost their houses. Some
are still living in trailers. It was really a team effort. It sounds like such as
cliche, but I don't think that every organization acted like we did. We
honestly came to work for each other and there was never a concern about
rank. I had teachers making major decisions; I had directors telling deputy
superintendents what they needed to do, and everybody just shed their
titles and their turf. . . . The effort was incredible. We were accessible. It
didn't turn into this bunker mentality. Every senior staff person was out
there. Every senior staff person was part of the process. I had senior staff
people registering people in the tent city, in Harris Field. I had auditors
handling the volunteer line. All titles, all job descriptions were set aside.
We did what we had to get the job done. (Visiedo Interview)

Within a few days following the storm, Visiedo had set up a telephone service called the HelpLine under the direction of Deputy Superintendent Marilyn Neff that provided information on the recovery effort
and the reopening of the schools. Following the hurricane, a total of
12,000 calls were received and answered by the HelpLine in a period of
less than two weeks.[11]

Efforts such as the HelpLine, while largely symbolic, were important in terms of providing the community with a sense that things would
return to normal and that despite delays efforts were underway to overcome the crisis caused by the storm.

Visiedo's efforts and those of his staff were among the most visible
signs of rebuilding that occurred in the first days and weeks after the
storm—a fact widely recognized throughout the community. As he
proudly explained:

We get criticized for a lot of things and deservedly so. But the fact of the
matter is we did a hell of a job. We transported people before and after the
storm. We were the ones that brought this community back together by
opening up the schools. We had forty-four schools that looked like they
weren't going to open. We ended up with ten. Everybody had a school to
go to. When the schools opened up on September 14, it was like a new
chapter opened up in this community.[12]

Throughout the first few weeks there was constant skepticism as to
whether or not the schools would actually be able to reopen:

Nobody gave us credit. Every day I got asked the question, "Do you really
think that you are going to open up September 14?" It was like a focus
going from a support organization right after the hurricane . . . helping peo-

ple, transporting people, sheltering people, feeding people . . . to the primary mission of the organization. The whole focus was on, "Can we get the kids in school?" Everything else was secondary. If we had not done it, or if we had done it and caused complete chaos, the setback to this community would have been tremendous. The fact is that we did deliver. We did open. That was a huge step in progress. To this day, you go to South Miami Heights, you look around the neighborhood, there is garbage everywhere, trees, trash. You look at that school—the yard is manicured, the flowers, it's clean. It's the center of civilization in a very small area. That's critical. The psychological impact of that, even though you're always going to have somebody who is angry about something. [That] you can drop off your kid, in the midst of this destruction, to a manicured, clean building is something that people sort of accept. But the work that is associated with that and the impact that it has is tremendous. That's what we did. [13]

DAMAGE TO THE SCHOOLS

All 287 Dade County Public Schools suffered some damage as a result of the storm. While most of the serious damage occurred in the southern half of the county, over 400 school-owned facilities had to be inspected and assessed before the schools could reopen. Early estimates indicated that the school system had suffered $300 million in losses with nine schools destroyed and twenty-three suffering heavy damage.[14] These figures were later revised to somewhere between $190 to $210 million. Examples of property damage included exterior and interior finishes, roofing, electrical and mechanical systems, fencing, and landscaping. Property contents damage included library books and equipment; computer equipment; PBX communications and television relay equipment; textbooks; furniture and office equipment; science laboratory equipment; records and documentation; and classroom supplies.[15]

The damage assessment process would have been a monumental task under normal circumstances, but it was further complicated as a result of storm related problems. Telephone and electrical services were lost completely or severely disrupted throughout the county for the first week and much longer than that in many neighborhoods in the southernmost part of the county. Cellular emergency phones worked only on a haphazard basis, because the towers that relayed their messages had been damaged or destroyed. Heavy rains, following the hurricane, made getting temporary roofs in place not only more difficult but also absolutely essential. Coordinating damage assessment efforts, however, proved to be extremely difficult. Shortages of supplies, transportation problems, the need for and lack of skilled workers, all contributed to delays and complications.

Shortly after the storm, Superintendent Visiedo described some of the damage as being "incredible" with schools such as Perrine Elementary looking "as if it had been hit by a missile."[16] R. R. Moton in Homestead was almost completely destroyed, having suffered a collapsed roof and walls, as well as damage from looting. Arvida Middle School had lost its entire roof, and the inside of the school had been subjected to extensive water damage.[17] Air Base Elementary School not only had suffered physical damage but also smelled so badly because of food that had rotted in the cafeteria, that workers had to put on surgical masks before they could begin to work on the school.[18]

FEDERAL INVOLVEMENT IN THE
REBUILDING PROCESS

Federal troops contributed significantly to the cleanup effort of the schools. On Labor Day, for example, 700 Navy Seabees worked the entire day clearing debris from football fields and playgrounds, replacing roofs, and cleaning interiors for schools located in the southern half of the county.[19] Foreign military personnel also contributed to the process. At Mays Middle School a contingent from a Canadian naval ship put a new roof on the school.

The military's relief effort had a positive impact. It cast them in a new role both for the communities they were helping and even for themselves. As Navy Petty Officer Charles Hair explained: "This is hard work, but this is better than going to war. It feels good to be here helping our own people."[20]

Federal assistance for the schools came from groups other than the military. The U.S. Department of Education, for example, dispatched 100 employee volunteers for a minimum of ten days each to help with relief efforts. In addition, the President and Congress channeled $40 million from contingency funds to help the school system with transportation and operating costs following the storm.[21]

On October 3, 1992, Superintendent Visiedo submitted a request to President George Bush for $85.9 million in federal hurricane relief funding for the schools. This included $12.5 million for special educational programs and curriculums for high schools in hurricane affected areas; $50 million to lower student-teacher ratios and provide special supplies in the hurricane related area; $5 million to provide outreach and counseling services for teachers and staff affected by the hurricane; $1 million for extended after school care for children; $2 million for increased security after the military departed; $7 million for a hurricane recovery office; $3 million for the enhancement of student services (school psychologists, visiting teachers, etc.) in the devastated region; $1 million for additional transportation services; $5.2 million for lower classroom teacher-pupil ratios in adult education programs; and finally, $10 million for health care and social services on site at hurricane impacted schools.[22] These requests had all been coordinated beforehand with Secretary of Education Lamar Alexander and his staff.[23] At a press conference on October 14, 1992, Alexander promised to deliver a total of $82 million to help rebuild the schools.[24]

HELP COMES FROM
ELSEWHERE IN THE COUNTRY

Undoubtedly, one of the main effects of the comprehensive and almost instantaneous national and international media coverage of the storm was that many people from across the country and even throughout the world reached out and sent relief supplies and aid workers to South Florida. During the first days and weeks after the storm, convoys of supply trucks and assistance teams came in a continuous stream down through Florida to south Dade County. Despite the tremendous need for supplies, emergency operation groups and the government were not prepared to deal with the storage and distribution of the huge amount of materials that arrived following the storm; neither were there preparations to accommodate the workers who came from across the country to assist in the rebuilding process.

Clothing, food, and other supplies were often damaged or completely destroyed as the result of an inadequate distribution system and procedures. In the first few weeks after the storm, huge mounds of unsorted clothing were a common sight in the emergency relief shelters and schools. At Ruben Dario Middle School, which we visited shortly after the storm, thousands of pieces of clothing and hundreds of boxes of canned goods and paper products were stacked in the auditorium, far from the worst hit areas where they were badly needed.

People were extremely generous in their desire to reach out to the schools that had been affected by the storm. Nationwide, 600 schools contacted the Dade County Public School System (DCPS) about providing clothing and supplies to hurricane damaged schools.[25]

In retrospect, because of distribution procedures already in place, the school system seemed better able to organize and make effective use of contributions from the outside than many other South Florida agencies. Additional emergency procedures established by the schools to deal with contributions should provide useful models for future disaster preparedness. It is interesting to note that in the 1926 hurricane the problem of receiving emergency supplies was much more directly handled by local government officials, who made it very clear that they would only initially take certain specific items such as tents, cots, bedding, and limited amounts of clothing.[26] Later, when more specific items were needed, requests were sent out for additional assistance. Perhaps controlling the flow of contributions and assistance was a much easier task when Miami was a smaller community.

CHILDREN TRANSFERRED TO SCHOOLS
IN OTHER PARTS OF THE COUNTY
AND OUTSIDE OF DADE COUNTY

At the October 14, 1993 school board meeting, it was estimated that between 18,000 to 20,000 students (out of a total 317,000 students) had moved permanently out of the district as a result of the storm. Revenue losses based on state funding for full-time equivalent numbers of students were estimated at approximately $60 million.[27]

As of October 1992, because of students moving out of the county, the system had a surplus of 300 teachers. In addition, because of the destruction of businesses, it was estimated that projected revenue from property taxes would decline 4 percent as a result of the storm. This represented a total of $18.45 million in lost revenue for the system.[28] Deputy Superintendent Richard Hinds reported to the board that the school system, as a result of the storm, was experiencing the worse budget crisis in twenty years, with only $23 million in reserves out of a total budget of $1.6 billion.[29]

Just how drastically some schools were affected by out migration is indicated by school attendance figures. Most seriously affected were the following: Redland Elementary, with daily average enrollment down from 862 to 430; Chapman Elementary, down from 931 to 415; and Homestead Senior declining from 2,349 to 962.

In order to keep from terminating teachers, as well as to provide additional instructional support to schools in the hurricane affected area, an "Enhanced Instructional Support" program was put into place. This program was designed to provide greater individualized instruction, as well as to provide an opportunity to stabilize faculty in schools while students gradually returned to them. A total of forty-four elementary schools, ten middle schools, and three senior high schools would benefit from the program.[30]

Hurricane Andrew only served to compound problems of overcrowding and strained facilities that were already evident in the public schools before the hurricane. Schools in areas of the county that were not seriously affected by the storm, but that were already overcrowded before Andrew struck, found themselves with many new students. Charles Drew Elementary School in Liberty City, for example, had already reached its cap of 840 students but had to accept dozens of additional students immediately after the storm. American High School in Northwest Dade was already seriously overcrowded with 3,600 students yet had to absorb approximately 100 new students as a result of the hurricane.[38]

Braddock High School, which opened two years before the storm, was originally designed to house 3,100 students. During the 1992/93 school year, it had 5,100 students on a staggered schedule. Crowding in the school was not just a result of the hurricane. New housing developments in the area around the school had also contributed to the crowded conditions within the school. The storm, however, compounded problems. Not only were there significant numbers of new transfer students, but also the school's gymnasium and auditorium had been severely damaged by the storm, making them unusable for the school year.[32]

The movement of families with students from the southern part of the county to housing in the northern end created a series of storm related pressures in seemingly unaffected parts of the county. As Associate Superintendent Nelson Diaz explained:

> One of the problems that we have is that the people from the south have moved to the north part of the county. When we have schools that have

grown by 200 students since the hurricane, we can't say that they aren't affected by the hurricane. They aren't affected by damage, but they are affected by population increases that grew out of the storm.[40]

Transferring to new schools was often a difficult experience. Students found themselves separated from friends and school and community traditions. Eveline Betancourt, for example, an eleventh grader transferred to American High School in North Dade, insisted on ordering a class ring for her prehurricane school, Homestead High School, despite the fact that her family had permanently moved to the northern part of the county and had no intention of moving back south. As Betancourt explained: "I want to graduate with Homestead, go to the prom with Homestead . . . we're a big family. It's where I was raised."[34]

By January 1993, more than 30,000 students, approximately 10 percent of the student population, had either transferred out of South Dade schools or were unaccounted for in terms of school enrollments. Initially, school system officials assumed that many families would move back to their homes in South Dade after the Christmas holiday. This optimistic expectation was not to be realized, since housing was not repaired fast enough to make it possible for students to return in the numbers originally anticipated.[35]

DERAILING THE SCHOOL SYSTEM'S BUILDING PROGRAM

Hurricane Andrew caused a number of unanticipated problems for the school system and the community. Among the most significant was the effect of the storm on the $1.5 billion school building program. Renovations and additions were delayed on schools throughout the county as a result of the need to repair storm damaged schools. Even more important was the redistribution of students from the southern to the northern end of the county as a result of the storm. Construction scheduled for schools in the southern part of the county, such as for Peskoe and Country Walk Elementary Schools, suddenly became, at least for the time being, unnecessary due to the destruction of the local communities they served. As Superintendent Visiedo explained a few months after the storm:

> Projects that were pressing before are now not as important because of demographic changes. Country Walk was a community that badly needed a school. But now there's no community there. Clearly these are policy issues that must be decided by the board.[36]

In the case of Peskoe, which was half constructed at the time of the storm and intended to relieve overcrowding at Air Base, Leisure City, and Chapman Elementary Schools, the question arose as to whether or not the school should even open.

Prior to Hurricane Andrew, growth in the school system's student population was to the west (bounded by the Everglades) and the south (bounded by Biscayne Bay and Florida Bay), areas directly in the line of the storm. The main impact zone of the hurricane was in this high-growth area. Plans and commitments were already under way for building new schools and updating existing plants in the southern and western portions of the county (Dade County Public School District Regions five and six). Following the hurricane, school system officials found themselves facing the dilemma of trying to determine the extent to which the storm had caused people to permanently move out of these previously high-growth areas. Particularly difficult to deal with was the fact that if new schools were not built and established schools were not repaired, then parents and their children almost certainly would not return to the area. Even if the schools were constructed, however, it was not clear that people who had moved north after the storm would return.

Following the storm, the school system requested, as part of FEMA—Federal Emergency Management Assistance—a total of 600 portables classrooms. They were assured of receiving 345. According to school system officials, FEMA was unwilling to fund the additional 255 portables because it was felt that the request reflected population shifts within the district and was not a result of hurricane damage. The school system argued that while schools in the northern part of the county did not need portables because of storm damage, their over-crowding was in fact a direct result of the storm.

School system officials also faced the problem of determining who was responsible for reimbursements and assistance. As in the question of who should pay for portable classrooms and why, there was considerable cause for debate. The impact of these decisions would prove to be absolutely critical, since a total of over $87.5 million was requested from the federal government to help the schools in the recovery process.

Federal funds were used to replace schools with 50 percent or more damage as a result of Hurricane Andrew. Two schools immediately fit this designation: Redland and Caribbean Elementary Schools. In the case of Redland, the school had earlier been designated as a historical landmark requiring the maintenance of as much of its original historic structure as possible. The school system and the federal government debated over whether or not R. R. Moton Elementary School should be awarded federal rebuilding monies, since only 48 percent of its damage could be attributed to the storm. In fact, Moton had sustained additional damage as a result of the looting and vandalism that followed the storm. School system officials argued that this damage would not have occurred if the hurricane had not made the school vulnerable to vandals. They cited the precedent of the Los Angeles Unified School District receiving federal replacement assistance for schools that were damaged during the riots in the spring of 1992.

The question of whether or not damages from looting and vandalism were the responsibility of local or federal agencies reflects just one of the many complex issues that came into play when trying to determine actual damages and losses from the storm. Other issues also created a difficult situation for school officials. For example, as part of the December 16, 1992 DCPS School Board meeting, ninety-four parents from the devastated Country Walk housing complex requested a hearing concerning the development of their school. The schools had been planned for their community prior to the hurricane, and they wanted the plan to be given the go-ahead for construction. The community's desire for a guarantee that the school would be built created a serious dilemma for the school system. On one level, approving the construction would reconfirm the school system's commitment to serving and helping in the rebuilding process in the southern part of the county. On the other hand, the emerging needs of the increasingly overcrowded northern part of the county could not be overlooked.

Henry Fraind, Assistant Superintendent for District Office Management, Operations, and Communications, and the school system's chief spokesperson, in addressing the need for public reassurance about the rebuilding of the school system in the southern part of the county, explained that:

> New schools have to be built as quickly as possible. The community feels that we're going to forget about the south. Therefore, the youngsters and parents that moved north may be reluctant to move back. If we don't act quickly, we are going to destroy the entire school system.[37]

Yet, establishing construction priorities was not as easy as one might think. Prior to the hurricane, there had been a building slump in Dade

County. The school system's massive building project represented the largest source of construction income available to contractors in the county. Bids for school construction and renovations were highly competitive and seldom overbudget. With the hurricane, however, demands on the building industry were so great that the school system found itself, for the first time in years, having to significantly increase the price it paid for construction. School system officials were faced with the fact that renovation and new construction costs had suddenly skyrocketed. Following the storm, estimates increased by approximately 30 percent—increased costs included not just materials but also labor.

After the storm most construction bids had to be rejected because they came in well over architects' estimates. However, by not building, the message—not necessarily the one that the school system wanted to communicate—that went out to the community was that the rebuilding process in the south would not necessarily be supported.

Sally Osborne, State Department of Education liaison for the district, explained: "We're having to reject bids that are coming in. Posthurricane bids are all over budget. Prior hurricane bids were very seldom overbudget." (ODFS Interview) Although prior building contracts were locked in, contractors now faced the difficulty of getting materials. In addition, increased demands placed on local builders made completing contracts more difficult. Time delays occurred in all of the projects that were under construction prior to the storm.

PLANNING FOR FUTURE DISASTERS

Hurricane Andrew provided some particular lessons on how to deal with similar disasters in the future. Many of the problems that emerged for the school system during the rebuilding process involved bureaucratic procedures. Osborne explained, for example, that the school system needed to set up a procedure that would make it possible to collect the necessary data to receive reimbursement for expenses incurred as a result of the hurricane:

> What is happening right now is that we are going through a tremendous process of capturing all of the information. We didn't have the infrastructure in place. The government is asking us for an unbelievable amount of detail—canceled checks. They want to see invoices and names. In the transportation area we didn't keep track of the numbers of hours that peo-

ple worked in transportation or maintenance. We have good records, but we don't have a process for capturing that information in order to show it to FEMA or the Red Cross. It's unbelievable the amount of time that we have had to spend getting this data. Next time around, hopefully, there won't be a next time around, we will be set up in-house where we have the data and the system to track all of the repairs, all of the vehicles, all of the locations, all of the communication. . . . I'd like to see us construct an information system. Someone at a high level position needs to be in charge of donations. We received a lot of stuff. Some of it we really couldn't use. Some people sent us books that were thirty years old. They meant well, but some of the materials were useless. IBM sent us a $5 million donation. It came into another bureau and the way that it was being distributed was not really the way it should have been. I think that has to change; a central clearing house has to be set up. We got a call from the Port of Miami, and I don't know how many cases of textbooks they had. We had warehouses full of things and not the manpower to sort through it to distribute it. We didn't know who had sent them or why. Some people used this occasion to clear their warehouses . . . There has to be a chain of command, a plan of book keeping that is required to document the damage assessment, debris removal, the counting and book keeping that is required. We haven't ever had to deal with tasks as monumental as this. We have never had to deal with FEMA. (ODFS Interview)

The need to have fully functioning communication systems was seen as being essential to dealing with the emergency process. As Osborne explained:

We are investigating our own communication system. Metro Dade has their own. We're thinking about having some cells around town. We can't get reimbursed by FEMA, we'll have to invest in it ourselves. We need communication with our construction department. That's what caused the delays. We couldn't coordinate anything. With no ability to coordinate, then you get back to transportation and the large geographical area that we are dealing with and you get somebody down in Florida City trying to communicate about generators that are functional but with water dripping on them. You have an emergency situation where a lot of people could get shocked. You need something right then to keep the water off. We were in gridlock with no way to communicate. (ODFS Interview)

Communication and effective transportation in the end were crucial in trying to cope with the crisis caused by the storm. Simply getting workmen to where they needed to go to do emergency repairs was a major problem:

The traffic lights were not functioning and there was no simple way to get anywhere. What would be a half-hour ride would take three hours. By the time a workman would get to a site, it would be time to come back. It might be 9:00 before they would get finished. Transportation was very difficult, if not impossible, for the first few days. Just traveling would take the whole day. It might be easier to travel by helicopter. But you have to be careful there too. There was a lot of traffic in the air. (ODFS Interview)

According to Osborne, despite the problems of heavy air traffic, having the ability to do assessments of the situation by air really helped. In the end, however, having effective centralized leadership was for her the critical factor in how successful the emergency efforts were after the storm. She also realized that "when it is all said and done, you really can't plan for a disaster." (ODFS Interview)

CONCLUSION

In effect, the Dade County Public Schools, like other government agencies in the county, had no substantial or comprehensive hurricane disaster plans in place when Hurricane Andrew struck. The valiant efforts of school officials, community leaders and citizens throughout the district, were not sufficient to organize the effort required to make the rapid and massive recovery that was ultimately needed to survive the storm without major trauma.

In spite of the lack of a fully prepared system, the informal responses that emerged proved to be critical in the early stages of the rebuilding process. The fact that the schools were able to open on September 14, only a few weeks after the storm, is a testament to the extraordinary dedication and effort of the employees. Many of the lessons learned as a result of the storm served to enhance the district's capacity for effective and decisive responses. This learning process should serve the district well in preparing for and responding to other potential emergencies in the near future. The experience of the Dade County Public Schools should also serve as a model for other schools around the country.

NOTES

1. See Louis M. Smith and William Geoffrey, *The Complexities of an Urban Classroom: An Analysis Toward a General Theory of Teaching* (New York: Holt, Rinehart and Winston, 1968), p. 21.

2. Dade County School Board Status Report, Broadcast over WLRN Radio, August 28, 1992.

3. Lisa Getter, "Loss of 15 Homes Unites Family of 65," *Miami Herald*, August 27, 1992, p. 2B.

4. Ibid, p. 26. Schools that functioned as Red Cross shelters included Arvida Middle School, Citrus Grove Middle School, Greenglade Elementary School, Hialeah-Miami Lakes High School, Hialeah Middle School, James Bright Elementary School, Jose Marti Middle School, Lake Stevens Elementary School, Lake Stevens Middle School, Lorah Park Elementary School, McMillan Middle School, Miami Gardens Elementary School, Miami Carol City High School, Miami Coral Park High School, Miami Lakes Elementary School, Miami Lakes Middle School, Miami Lakes Technical Center, North Miami Beach High School, Norwood Elementary School, Palm Springs North Elementary School, Richmond Heights Elementary School, Royal Green Elementary School, and Skyway Elementary School.

5. Interview with Nelson Diaz conducted by Sandra H. Fradd and Eugene F. Provenzo, Jr., December 16, 1993, Miami, Florida.

6. Interview with Octavio Visiedo conducted by Eugene F. Provenzo, Jr., March 14, 1993, Miami, Florida. The following series of quotes are from the Visiedo interview and are cited.

7. Jon O'Neill and Marcia Smith, "School's In for Seekers of Shelter," *Miami Herald*, September 2, 1992, p. 13A.

8. For background on Visiedo's role during the hurricane see Marilee C. Rist, "Miami's Iron Man," *Executive Educator* (March 1993): pp. 29-32.

9. Ibid, p. 4L.

10. Interview with Octavio Visiedo conducted by Eugene F. Provenzo, Jr., March 14, 1993, Miami, Florida (henceforth called Visiedo interview).

11. DCPS (Dade County Public Schools) Board Minutes, September 9, 1993., p. 6.

12. Ibid.

13. Ibid.

14. "Andrew by the Numbers," *Miami Herald*, September 24, 1992, p. 1.

15. School Board of Dade County, Minutes of the October 14, 1992 School Board Meeting (Conference Session re: "Dade County Public Schools Hurricane Andrew Action Plan," p. 6.

16. Jon O'Neill, "South Dade Schools Face Major Repairs," August 30, 1992, p. 18C.

17. Ibid.

18. John O'Neil, Ana Acle, and Patrick May, "Dade Schools Bracing for the First Day," *Miami Herald*, September 10, 1992, p. 1B.

19. Lydia Martin, "Seabees Help Schools Get Shipshape Again," *Miami Herald*, September 8, 1992, p. 1B; and Pitsch, Mark, "Down But Not Out, Patched Dade Schools Open," *Education Week*, Vol. XII, #3, September 23, 1992, p. 15.

20. Martin, "Seabees Help Schools," p. 1B.

21. Karne Diegmueller and Mark Pitsch, "Hurricane Deals Harsh Blow to Fla., La. Schools," *Education Week*, Vol. XII, #1, September 9, 1992, p. 22.

22. Dade County Public Schools, *Hurricane Andrew Recovery Plan* (Miami: Dade County Public Schools, October 14, 1992), pp. i-iii.

23. Ibid, p. iii.

24. Tom Dubocq, "U.S. Promises Dade Schools All Aid Needed," *Miami Herald*, October 15, 1993, p. 1B.

25. O'Neil, Acle, and May, "Dade Schools Bracing," p. 1B.

26. L. F. Reardon, *The Florida Hurricane and Disaster* (Miami: Centennial Press, 1992), p. 16.

27. School Board of Dade County, Minutes of the October 14, 1992 School Board Meeting. Conference Session re: "Dade County Public Schools Hurricane Andrew Action Plan," p. 2.

28. Ibid, p. 3.

29. Ibid, p. 2.

30. Ibid, p. 4.

31. O'Neil, Acle, and May, "Dade Schools Bracing," p. 1B.

32. Cristina I. Pravia and Jon O'Neill, "Split Decisions: Students, Teachers Make Best of Staggered Schedules," *Miami Herald*, Neighbors Section, January 10, 1993, pp. 18.

33. Interview with Nelson Diaz conducted by Sandra Fradd and Eugene F. Provenzo, Jr., December 16, 1992, Miami, Florida.

34. Tom Dubocq, "Storm-displaced Students Deal with Devastated Past," *Miami Herald*, January 3, 1993, p. 1B.

35. Dubocq, "Storm-displaced Students Deal," p. 2B.

36. Jon O'Neill, "School Construction in a Jumble," October 20, 1992, p. 1b.

37. Interview with Sally Osborne, Nelson Diaz, Henry Fraind, and Jerry Salcines conducted by Sandra H. Fradd and Eugene F. Provenzo, Jr., Miami, Florida, December 16, 1992. The following series of quotes are from the Osborne, Diaz, Fraind, and Salcines interview (henceforth called ODFS Interview) and are cited in the text.

3

The Immediate Impact of
Hurricane Andrew on Families
and Children in South Florida

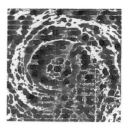

Hurricane Andrew was a traumatic experience for nearly everyone in South Florida. For children, it was a particularly unsettling event. Many children experienced the storm huddled with members of their families in closets or in some central and windowless hallway, their only protection the mattresses over their bodies as the storm broke into their homes. Many will live with the memory and terror of the storm for the rest of their lives.

In this chapter we deal with the experiences of children and families during and after the storm. These first person stories provide insight into the difficulties that teachers and administrators faced in reestablishing the school program after the hurricane.

In the south part of the county, elementary teachers have often described to us how they can walk into a classroom and see children become visibly agitated and upset if the wind suddenly rises or if there is a heavy rain. Tony Proscio, a *Miami Herald* editor, expressed the fears many children would potentially carry with them into adulthood, when he described how:

> In the black silence of some future night, in a quiet bedroom where (God willing) the ceilings will be dry and the wall sound, where crickets chirp under a moonlit window, a child will nonetheless jerk awake, certain in the knowledge that there really *are* monsters under the bed, that loving parents and sturdy walls do not bring safety, that the world is a random and hostile place where the horror is vast and nameless and always just beyond shore.[1]

The types of experiences children actually went through as a result of Hurricane Andrew were widely described in newspaper interviews published immediately after the storm and in essays written by children on their return to the school in September. Charles Agero, III, an eleven year-old in Kendall explained how during the storm:

I thought it was going to be scary and everything, but it was more scarier than I thought. It was hot and you could hear the wind outside. We were sleeping in the hallway. The roof did come off. We were lucky, because there's a bunch of houses worse than us."[2]

Four-year old Lakira Mills from Naranja told her mother that "a monster was at the window." Madeline Figueroa, another eleven year-old from Kendall explained that she thought that the storm:

was going to come and it was going to blow our house away and we were going to die. I slept in my parents' room. When it started, I heard it and woke up and I was scared. (from "After the Storm. . . .)

In many schools after the storm children wrote about their experiences and what happened to them and their families. Fourth graders at Caribbean Elementary School who had lost their school and been reassigned on double-session with South Miami Heights Elementary School, wrote notes to children in Wisconsin thanking them for letters and care packages that had been sent to them following the storm. These letters were shared with us by their teachers before they were mailed. They give a clear sense of the immediacy and profound impact of the hurricane on the individual lives of the children.

Carey Tait, a boy nine years of age, wrote:

During the hurricane we were in the bathroom hoping we would make it. Early in the morning we heard someone knocking on the door. My dad went and answered it. The people knocking on the door were our neighbors. They came over because they lost their roof. We all went to see what happened to our house. It was a mess. Five of our roofs caved in. There was broken glass everywhere. When we walked we were walking in water puddles. (from "After the Storm. . . .)

Rosa Golde wrote that "when Hurricane Andrew hit we were in the bathroom. In the room we were scared. It messed up the world."

Lavern Martin described how "during Hurricane Andrew we were hiding in my sister's room. Then her room caved-in. There was a flood in the house and the road was full of water. The road looked like a sea". Digna Quezada simply said that "the hurricane was not good. We did not have fun. The trees fell. My home fell. I did not like Hurricane Andrew. My school fell too. I did not like to see my school fall." Shana McPherson wrote: Hurricane Andrew destroyed our homes, school, and our personnel things. We miss everything that is gone." (from "After the Storm. . . .)

Yadira Caraballo wrote: "[My family and I] spent the hurricane in my grandmother's house. It was very scary. We had to run to a closet. Six people went in a little closet. My dog was in the closet too. We came out safe. None of us got hurt." Racquel Santiago described what happened after her father woke her up at the height of the storm: "Within five to seven minutes the windows blew in my room and brother's room. Then we went to the bathrooms, the girls in one and the boys in the other. Everything was moving. Then, when the hurricane stopped and went away, we saw everything was destroyed. Then the army came and helped us." (from "After the Storm. . . .)

After the storm, children in the southern half of the county were introduced to a confusing and alien world. Within a few days, the military were everywhere—with their uniforms, guns, and trucks clearly present. Children who had never seen a soldier before now saw them at every street corner and at every intersection. Familiar landmarks were blown away and neighborhoods that had been leafy and inviting were now stark and barren.

Friends disappeared without a goodbye, moving into other parts of the county or even out of the state. For the older children, football season was put on hold, and dreams of homecomings and senior proms were shattered, as the normal patterns of school and community were disrupted. Typical was Addie Adair, a senior at Homestead Senior High School, who was sent to Cooper City High School in Broward County after the storm. As she explained, "I planned so much for this year and now it's been taken away."[3]

THE PSYCHOLOGICAL IMPACT
OF THE STORM ON CHILDREN

Parents, teachers, community leaders, and counselors were faced with the problem of how to help children after the storm. Tony Proscio asked what we can say to reassure a child about the future after she has experienced the uncertainty of a hurricane such as Andrew:

> What do we say to such a child? Surely not that her terrors are healthy, that they will improve her sense of foreign policy and military priorities, that they should inspire her to become an engineer and design safer roofs. "At night," my friend says, "I tell my daughter that we'll have trouble for a time, but then life will be better, and we'll be safe in a new

home, with new toys and dry clothes and a tree in the yard. But I can see she doesn't believe me, and she can tell I'm not so sure myself.[4]

Emergency psychological services were provided to adults and children by the Red Cross and other groups immediately after the storm. Typical of the experience of counselors was that of Janine Shelby, a doctoral student in counseling psychology at the University of Miami. Shelby worked as a volunteer member of the Emergency Disaster Mental Health Services Team in Perrine right after the storm. Over a three week period she was involved in approximately 170 therapy sessions with children, adults, and families.

Shelby worked primarily with African-American and Hispanic populations in the south part of the county. Most of the people with whom she worked had no portable radios, generators, or televisions for their homes. Cut off from the outside world and uninformed about what was happening around them, many were highly disoriented and frustrated. As Shelby described the situation, the people with whom she worked:

> had experienced a profound sense of loss, of personal possessions, of safety and of the control of their environment. . . . They had gone through the first stage of recovery—the euphoria of having survived the hurricane, and realized that their communities had become places of anger, fear, and suspicion. The sense of community had evaporated.[5]

Coping with the storm and its aftermath was even more difficult for the children, Shelby observed, than for the adults. As she explained:

> Because children have the conscious awareness of adults and they don't have experience in using coping strategies like adults do, children become the unrecognized victims [of the disaster]. . . . Children are in a state of self-identification and awareness and may be at greater risk of emotional difficulties. The ones they use [coping strategies] may fail quickly and easily, and there may be no more to replace them. Even if they are successful, the children may not have any way to measure success in what's happening because children tend to live in the present. (Shelby Interview)

Immediately following the storm, the media offered suggestions to parents to help children cope. A great deal of emphasis was placed on children talking through their experiences. Children relocated to the tent cities in South Dade, for example, were often encouraged by counselors and other adults to revisit the storm in conversations and drawings.[6] Parents were advised after the storm to discuss with their children what happened during the hurricane. If children were reluctant to talk, it was suggested that they could use stuffed animals and puppets to work through their experiences. Parents were also advised to have children draw pictures of the hurricane and to discuss the feelings that they had about what they drew.[7]

Despite common sense advice like this, Shelby pointed out

> that encouraging children to talk may increase their sense of anxiety and lack of resolution. Trying to talk when you really don't know what to say can add to the burden of frustration and failure. Talking may be counter-productive for some children who are still in a state where they are trying to resolve their difficulties.[8]

Shelby made clear that based upon her experience and the research that was available from the field, the tendency of schools and lay counselors to have children talk about their feelings and to engage in activities, such as drawing pictures of the storm and filling in coloring books about the hurricane, might be counterproductive:

> If they can't talk about their anxiety, and the adult in charge is asking them to do so, the children may have an even greater sense of frustration and negative self-identification than they would have had if the adult had done nothing. The schools tend to draw everything out at once, thinking that by doing this that they can bring resolution. Talking puts things in the past and makes it over. But the trauma is not over. It is ongoing. . . . Finding out what's really bothering children is a different approach than what's been typically happening in the schools. There's a need that the hurricane interventions don't provide. What the color books that are out there tend to do is give some explanation of the hurricane—understanding a hurricane cognitively. They have the children draw the hurricane and talk about what their house looks like now after the hurricane. And, that's all. It seems that by doing this we open children up, but we don't do anything for them with the information. (Shelby Interview)

The school system was certainly aware from the beginning of the crisis that children would need to be provided services and special help, such as counseling, after-school care, and even help with clothing, food, and school supplies, long after the storm was over. In this context, the special counseling programs set up by the school system to cope with the psychological consequences of the storm were particularly noteworthy.

Joe Jackson, the Supervisor of Psychological Services for the Dade County Public Schools, explained how, after the storm, he and his staff immediately began a program to provide students with expanded psychological and counseling services. Every school psychologist in the public schools went through a debriefing process "dealing with short term reaction to stress, and related physical and emotional responses." In addition, more long-term problems were addressed, including post-traumatic stress disorder. Jackson and his staff found themselves asking:

> What should we be looking at? What should we be expecting? If you look at it carefully, you realize that long term stress is actually short term stress extended. Most people have the short term, but they don't have the long term stress because they have gone through the (healing) process. If you still have it after 5 or 6 months, you are in post traumatic stress disorder.[9]

During the first few weeks following the hurricane, offers of assistance came from all over the country. Jackson explained how he and his staff were overwhelmed by "the amount of material and the number of people who wanted to help." Yet, before he and the school system could accept help from the outside, it was essential that the situation be surveyed and understood from within. As he explained:

> You have got to get a hold of the situation. But the situation is so massive, there are so many issues, and so many people to deal with that you have a tendency to pull within. People from outside [are] wanting to help, and you want to be able to help too, because we all work together helping people. But at the same time, we have to get our act together. We thanked them for offering help. It was very tough, but we said, "Be there in case we need you." Most people understood that. There were some who didn't. (Jackson Interview)

As Jackson concluded: "Sometimes it's better to work through a problem than to have someone hand you the answer on a plate." (Jackson Interview) Jackson and members of his staff made sure that special psychological services were available whenever a school needed them. Many schools did not request these services. As Jackson explained, services were asked for

> school by school, faculty by faculty. There were some situations where they said, "There are no problems here. Don't bother us." So we didn't send anybody out. They were almost bothered that we were telling them that they had problems. It was a business as usual type situation. (Jackson Interview)

According to Jackson, some principals were not completely aware of the problems that many of their students and faculty were dealing with:

> Many of the principals didn't understand what was happening in their faculties. . . . Some still don't understand. There are situations that I am aware of recently in a couple of our high schools in the south end of the county that the staff are telling me that the problems of the kids and the faculty are way greater than you can possibly imagine. (Jackson Interview)

Problems that existed in the schools prior to the hurricane were "doubled or quadrupled" after the storm, as children who were already causing problems before the storm simply got worse:

> It looks like we're dealing with kids who already have problems and that now they have more problems. . . . I am sure that there are kids who have problems now who didn't have problems before the storm. (Jackson Interview)

According to Jackson, after the storm many children simply moved down a level in terms of their ability to cope and work through their problems. The psychologists on his staff consistently reported to him that the children they were seeing were the students who also often had problems before the storm.

> An example is the kids who had been identified as emotionally handicapped. Now they are being identified as severely emotionally disturbed. They have jumped up a notch as far as the problems they are creating, and they are creating a lot of problems in the schools. (Jackson Interview)

The need for counseling and support services was not limited to just the storm affected areas. Many teachers who taught in the north end of the county lived in South Dade. In addition, children who were forced to move out the south end of the county into the north often needed special help:

> You have a group of people who have lost their homes who are working all over the county, not just in the south end of the county. Up in the north end you have a small percentage, 10-15 percent, who were in the storm. You have a pocket of parents who have moved up to the north end of the district, and also a pocket of teachers who have lost their homes. When I have gone out and spoken to those groups, [they say] "It's like everybody is ignoring us. They are saying that we don't have problems. . . ." They are really hurting but people are ignoring them. So they are appreciative of our coming out to speak to them. Those are definitely some issues that people have. (Jackson Interview)

Sometimes, receiving too much attention and help posed a problem for survivors from the south end of the county who had moved north:

> There have been a couple of situations that have been the other way. People got identified as victims, and every time they turned around someone would be saying: "Here's our victims. Let's help our victims." (Jackson Interview)

For Jackson, the problems caused by Hurricane Andrew would remain for a long time to come:

> With this natural disaster, it is something that we are going to be dealing with for five to ten years from now. Every time that you are driving though the community, you see places that are still torn up. . . . Every time that you go into that community, you experience somewhat of a short-term stress reaction because you are seeing what happened there, either in your own life or you are driving into it and seeing it. I don't think that anyone really knows what is going on with the long-term stress. I don't know if anyone has ever taken a look at what it does to people in the long-term to keep coming into it—other than maybe war zones—maybe like Nicaragua, where you could look at the long term effects. That may be the closest that we come to replicating what we have here. (Jackson Interview)

For Jackson, there was clearly the need for principals and administrators to adapt and break from traditional rules and procedures when necessary:

> Some administrators are more supportive and understanding of the faculty than others. It may be the personality of the principals and the way they were trained. A teacher may say on Monday, "I have to be at home on Friday for a building inspection." One administrator will see that as something requiring assistance, covering the classes. Another will see it as trying to get out of work. I just read an article about how important it is to make the focus on the employees. For most businesses, the focus is the customer. This book was stating the exact opposite. The number one focus has to be the employees. If it is the employees, then the employees will make the focus on the customers. If you go out of your way to make your employees feel good, then they will be more competent and capable in working with the customers. (Jackson Interview)

Students and their families were perceived as the customers whom the administration and teachers needed to serve. The school system, in order to have student needs served, needed to make sure that the people—i.e., the teachers and administrators who were serving them—were also OK and taken care of.

From a psychological point of view, opening the schools provided one of the first major steps in reestablishing traditional norms and something like the community that had existed before the storm. The role of the schools in the rebuilding process was clearly outlined by Jackson:

> Immediately after we opened the schools on the 14th of September—it was a breath of fresh air for the community. We were so fearful that we were going to get a whole bunch of kids falling apart. We had to be ready and go out of our way to focus on addressing their needs. What we found was the kids walked through the doors with the best clothes they ever had on in their lives and they were happy to be there. A lot of credit goes to the staff. I think that the school was the safest and securest place that those kids had. Parents were happy that they could send those kids to the schools for two reasons: 1. They didn't have to take care of the kids; and 2. parents realized that they couldn't provide as safe and secure a place for the children as the schools could. . . . We did it as quickly as we possibly could. The fact that we did it as quickly as we did was remarkable and extremely helpful to the community. (Jackson Interview)

In looking to the future, Jackson explained that he and the school system could not necessarily predict how children would respond to the crisis imposed by the hurricane. For example, it was widely assumed that test scores would seriously decline as a result of the storm. But according to Jackson:

> We are hearing that in some schools, the kids are actually doing better in school now than they were doing before. I can't figure that one out, other than the fact that they are focused. (Jackson Interview)

In planning for the future, Jackson emphasized the need to have more specific guidelines and procedures established for dealing with a crisis like the hurricane. He also perceived the need to anticipate the psychological problems that would almost certainly emerge as children faced the 1993 hurricane season:

> One of the things that we have to think about is what are we going to do with the kids in the summer. Come June, we have hurricane season. Even if we don't talk about it, we have got to deal with some anxiety factors that I think are going to come out then. . . . I don't think that we had enough people in this town trained to deal with major disasters. I think that as a community I think we still did very well, but we were not ready. We were

not prepared to deal with what came. My biggest concern [is] we had not prepared a lot of information to prepare our administration to deal with the needs of faculty. It is important that they get that. (Jackson Interview)

PARENTS COPING WITH THE CRISIS FOR THEIR CHILDREN

Just how traumatic the hurricane was for many children and their families—not just during the storm but in the weeks and months after the storm—is revealed in an interview with Teddy Patel, the PTA (Parent Teachers Association) president at Pine Villa Elementary School. Patel and his family lost their home in the storm. He recalled the experience of the storm and its effect on his son, a third grader, as follows:

> About 5:00 in the morning the barricades that we had put up over the windows got ripped off and all the windows were blown in. Then a tree came crashing into my son's room. He was in shock. He cried, "My room! My room!" Basically all that survived of the house was one bedroom—the master bedroom. Everything else was totally destroyed.[10]

Patel's son could not comprehend everything that was happening. As Patel explained, he:

> was panicking to the extent that he was saying, "Daddy, please call 911." And we were saying, "911 isn't going to come out." At about 6:00 am, my mom called from New York and actually got through to us. My son grabbed the phone from me and, yelled, "Grandma, please call 911!" She called the Dade County emergency rescue. They told her to tell us to get a mattress and cover ourselves with it. (Patel Interview)

Later that morning, after the storm subsided, Patel's son went to sleep. According to his father, the boy woke up later that afternoon. His reaction was one of denial:

> He just wouldn't talk about it. He looked in his room. He went outside. Even now, he refuses to talk about it. We've tried getting him to talk. He will say something once in awhile, and he will only speak about what happened to his room. He only says that he was with my wife in the master bedroom saying a prayer. . . . Sometimes he may say that the ceiling in his room collapsed. That's all. He really doesn't want to talk about it. (Patel Interview)

In the months following the storm, Patel's son became much more difficult to live with. As his father observed:

> He throws temper tantrums. He snaps. He tries not to listen. We have to tell him something three or four times before he does it. Before he was very obedient. Every now and again he will let out a burst, "I want to go back to our house." (Patel Interview)

Patel's son was not alone in denying the severity of the storm. He and his wife put off looking for a new place to live until a week after the storm:

> At first we started saying that our house was liveable. But, the first Saturday after the hurricane, the rains came down. We realized that we really couldn't live there. Then we started looking for a place and got one two weeks later. We moved in a place that was for sale. We are renting with a option to buy. It's a condo. My son has nowhere to play. He feels cooped up. It's getting to us. We need a yard. I still go by the old house every day so he can see his friends. (Patel Interview)

Besides experiencing the physical violence of the storm and having their homes destroyed, many children found themselves physically and psychologically vulnerable after the hurricane because of looting. Particularly in areas isolated from police services in the southern part of the county, looters entered storm damaged houses and took whatever valuables they could get. Jeannine Shelby, for example, commented that to people whom she had counseled in the Perrine area:

> the threat of looters was very real. People reported many attempts that looters made to come in the houses. For example, one woman reported that she hit a looter over the head. Another said that as the National Guard would drive through the neighborhood, the looters would come right behind them because the looters knew the routines and the rounds that the Guard made. (Patel Interview)

In general, the hurricane was a profoundly disruptive experience for most children. Just how disruptive is indicated by the results of a survey of eighty-two children at Redondo Elementary School in Homested conducted in October 1992 by Jon Shaw, Director of Child and Adolescent Psychiatry at the University of Miami. Shaw's survey revealed that 83 percent of the children interviewed were afraid or upset when they thought about the hurricane. Sixty-nine percent of the students indicated that they felt that the hurricane interfered with their school work, while 64 percent indicated that it was more difficult for them to pay attention. A total of 67 percent said that they were more nervous and jumpy than they were before the hurricane. The same number—67 percent of the children—also indicated that they were having nightmares.[11]

INCREASED SUICIDE ATTEMPTS BY CHILDREN

Among the most disturbing outcomes of Hurricane Andrew was the marked increase in suicide attempts by elementary school children. In early March of 1993, *The Miami Herald* reported that more than a dozen elementary school children had tried to kill themselves in the two previous months. An eight year-old boy jumped in front of a school bus; a seven year-old jumped off of a second floor balcony at a school. According to Octavio Visiedo, Superintendent of the Dade County Public Schools, the number of elementary school children attempting suicide had increased from one or two per year to one or two a week.[12] Counselors also reported a marked increase in children talking about killing themselves—the reported number reaching fifty to sixty in December and January of 1993.[13]

Fortunately, despite suicide attempts and increased reports of the desire to die, no children actually killed themselves. Sources of despair among children included the pressures of rebuilding, relocation from familiar neighborhoods and schools, the loss of friends as a result of the scattering of families after the storm, the loss of recreational facilities, loneliness and boredom, and the fear that another hurricane might return soon.[14]

Perhaps children have always suffered more than adults in stressful situations where they know that something is wrong but they are unaware of appropriate responses to make in order to resolve the difficulties. During periods of stress and anxiety, families attempt to go about their lives as best they can. The time and attention that might normally be given to the needs of children necessarily goes to the problem at hand. In times of extreme stress, children are usually not consulted or involved in problem solving. Not fully informed or understanding what is taking place around them, children sense that their world is not right, but they are powerless to set things in order. Like children who have experienced previous disasters, the children who faced life after Andrew had vivid memories of the event. They were clearly aware of the damage and the ensuing chaos. What they may have lacked was a sense of responsibility and participation in the recovery process.

CONCLUSION

A disaster such as Hurricane Andrew is, in many respects, not that different from other natural or man-made traumas that have been experienced by children in the past. Hurricane Andrew was different from nearly any other previous disaster, however, in its magnitude. Perhaps never before in American history has such a large group of children experienced the same terror caused by a single event.

Isolated from the natural world that children of previous generations had lived in—more connected to media and the conveniences provided by electricity, such as air-conditioning—the disruption and trauma caused by Hurricane Andrew was almost certainly experienced at a different, and possibly more intense, level than that experienced by children who had gone through previous disasters but who had been raised to be more self-reliant and connected to the communities in which they lived.

We wonder if the trauma imposed by Hurricane Andrew may well be greater than is at first evident. We know that the storm induced great physical damage. It almost certainly also imposed great psychological stress on children—stress that we suspect will live with them for years to come and probably will not be fully understood by them, if ever, until they are well into adulthood. We wonder if Hurricane Andrew has left a generation of children in South Florida less confident in themselves and less secure about the place in which they live and the persons with whom they interact.

In this context, John Wolin has argued that the adults who survived Hurricane Andrew, have witnessed a "rebirth." We have been tested, and our sense of self and personal worth has been expanded. According to Wolin, "We've come to know that we love our homes, our trees, our neighborhoods much more than we imagined."[15] For the children of Andrew, however, they will never be able to shake a "feeling of loss. The land will fight back, will draw closer each year to the beauty we knew. But I do not believe the return will be complete in the time left to those of us known as adults."[16]

For the children who experienced Hurricane Andrew, many may never be able to shake the feeling of loss. Each time a dark cloud gathers in the sky, each time the thunder rumbles and the rain spills in torrents from the purple sky, they may wonder if they are to once again be engulfed by a disaster like Andrew.

NOTES

1. Tony Proscio, "What Do We Say to Our Children?" *Miami Herald*, September 8, 1992, p. 21a.

2. "After the Storm What Kids Say, What Kids Ask," p. 1E. The following quote in the text is cited and from this article.

3. Marilyn Marks, "Dade Teenagers Yearn for Return to Their Own Schools, Old Friends," *Miami Herald*, September 15, 1992, p. 3B.

4. Proscio, "What Do We Say?" p. 21A.

5. Interview with Janine Shelby conducted by Sandra H. Fradd, September 18, 1992, Miami, Florida.

6. Gail Epstein, "After Andrew Many Kids Are Talking, Drawing—Coping," September 18, 1992, p. 1E.

7. Monroe, Linda, "Helping Your Children Cope," *Miami Herald*, September 4, 1992, p. 2E.

8. Shelby interviewed by Fradd on September 18, 1992. The quote following is also from this interview.

9. Interview with Joe Jackson, conducted by Sandra H. Fradd and Eugene F. Provenzo, Jr., March 1, 1993, Miami, Florida. The following series of quotes are from this interview and cited in the text.

10. Interview with Teddy Patel conducted by Sandra H. Fradd and Eugene F. Provenzo, Jr., February 25, 1993, Miami, Florida. The following quotes are from this interview and cited in the text.

11. Lizette Alvarez, "Experts: Storm Survivors Suffer Combat Symptoms," *Miami Herald*, January 9, 1993, p. 1A.

12. John Donnelly, 'Andrew's Legacy: Kids Attempt Suicide," *Miami Herald*, March 7, 1993, pp. 1A, 12A.

13. Ibid, 12A.

14. Ibid.

15. John Wolin, "After Storm of Lifetime—a Rebirth," *Miami Herald*, May 23, 1993, p. 1G.

16. Ibid.

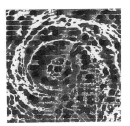

4

The Opening of the Schools—
Coping with the Aftermath

For all areas of southern Dade County, the process of rebuilding after Hurricane Andrew was painstakingly slow. Neighborhoods and communities responded to the storm and its aftermath differently. Two critical variables seemed to predict the pace with which the recovery process began: (a) geographical location, and (b) economic circumstances. Because of the scarcity of building supplies and financial resources, the poorest and the most hard hit areas were naturally slower to begin rebuilding. Middle and upper middle-class areas were able to marshal resources more quickly and within a few days after the storm were already showing the first signs of recovery. In this and subsequent chapters we discuss factors such as geographic location and socioeconomic status as affecting the rebuilding process, especially with respect to the schools.

Geographical location played an important role in the capacity of neighborhoods to rebuild. Starting at the northern edge of Coral Gables and continuing south on Dixie Highway (U.S. 1) to Homestead, the destruction caused by the storm became visibly worse. Large trees were uprooted and tiles broken on most roofs in Coral Gables. Greater damage occurred to apartment complexes and homes in the Kendall area. Even greater damage to the area of the Falls Shopping Center and below 136th Street. Moving to ground zero, the area around Perrine, Cutler Ridge, and Goulds presented a sight of almost total destruction. No building was left without severe damage. Most buildings in this area would require major reconstruction or have to be leveled.

In the most severe areas of destruction, almost every store, restaurant, and gas station—all the conveniences that are normally taken for granted—was gone. Once the roads were reopened after the storm, people living in these areas had to spend large amounts of time traveling to northern neighborhoods in the county where damage had been less severe, just to obtain basic necessities, such as food, water, gas, and building supplies.

In the areas where there were already established support systems, such as community action groups or, in the case of schools, strong parent involvement groups, such as the Parent Teacher Associations, the rebuilding process was also expedited. In those areas where there were more limited resources and a more limited infrastructure, the rebuilding process proceeded more slowly. As Joe Jackson, the Supervisor for Psychological Services for the Dade County Public Schools, explained:

> In families, as well as communities that were already well organized, the process of overcoming damage, both physical and psychological, moved forward. For those families, schools, or areas that were already experiencing difficulties, the trauma created by the storm was exacerbated and increased to such a degree that rebuilding and recovery might not be immediately possible.[1]

In this chapter, we look at the beginning of the 1992-93 school year. More specifically, in this and subsequent chapters, we look at the experience of students, teachers, administrators, and parents at three elementary schools profoundly affected by the Hurricane Andrew: Bowman Foster Ashe, Gilbert L. Porter, and Pine Villa. In doing so, we describe the rebuilding efforts in each of these schools and the factors that facilitated or inhibited the rebuilding process for each.

THE THREE SCHOOLS

Ashe is located a few miles north of Kendall Drive—the northern demarcation line of the area of South Dade County that was severely damages by Hurricane Andrew. Porter is located several miles south of Kendall Drive. Both schools border the eastern edge of the Everglades. These two modern schools provide a stark contrast to Pine Villa, which is located in the center of the most severely storm damaged part of the county.

Ashe and Porter are very new schools and serve upwardly mobile, middle-class suburban communities. Because both schools were designated as "Saturn" or innovative educational centers, they were special schools with staffs of hand-selected teachers. Each school site consisted of a series of buildings, composed of single-story structures in the front half, organized around a courtyard, and a two-story structure in the back. A fully equipped media center and physical education facilities contributed to a feeling of spaciousness and a gracious campus like setting—one often referred to as being "state of the art."

Pine Villa, composed largely of portables and an old central structure built in 1959, had been scheduled for renovation before the storm. Located in the economically disadvantaged area of Goulds, the school suffered major damage in the hurricane and was looted and vandalized after the storm.

All three schools have programs up through the fifth grade. For the 1991-92 school year, not including preschool programs, Ashe had a total of 841, Porter 982, and Pine Villa 1,185 students. Ashe and Porter were already close to their enrollment capacity. Neither school was assigned portable classrooms. Pine Villa exceeded its capacity of 664 students by 521 students. This overage of nearly 80 percent was handled by assigning the school twenty-five portable classrooms. Ashe and Porter had thirty-five and forty-two teachers respectively, while Pine Villa had a total of sixty teachers. Only three aides were assigned to Ashe and Porter, while Pine Villa had a total of twenty aides assigned to the school (see table 4.1). The reasons given by the school system for the larger number of teachers and aides at Pine Villa include the following: (a) the school has a Montessori magnet program and (b) the entire school is designated a Chapter 1 school and is thus eligible for a wide range of federal support.[2]

Although Pine Villa had the more limited physical plant, it was resource rich compared to the other two schools in terms of teacher aides and the overall student-teacher ratio. In addition, the teachers at Pine Villa had many more years of experience as indicated by their salary range; a significantly higher percentage of teachers were earning $42,000 or more. Important differences were found between Pine Villa and Ashe and Porter with respect to the educational background of their teachers. At Ashe and Porter, nearly 100 percent of the faculty and staff had at least a masters degree, whereas at Pine Villa slightly over half of this same group had masters degrees or higher (see table 4.1).

Wide variations existed between the three schools in terms of the demographic backgrounds of their student populations. Ashe was approximately 27 percent White non-Hispanic, 6 percent Black non-Hispanic, 65 percent Hispanic and 0 percent Asian or Native American. Porter was approximately 37 percent White non-Hispanic, 7 percent Black non-Hispanic, 51 percent Hispanic and 5 percent Asian or Native

American. Pine Villa was approximately 13 percent White non-Hispanic, 78 percent Black non-Hispanic, 8 percent Hispanic and 1 percent Asian or Native American. It is important to note that in the case of Ashe and Porter, the percentage of each ethnic group is consistently distributed across the school's various grade levels. At Pine Villa, ethnic distributions change across grades since White non-Hispanic and Hispanic students attracted to the Montessori program constitute a larger proportion of the pre-kindergarten, kindergarten, and first grade students, while the Black non-Hispanic students represent a higher proportion of the students in the third, fourth, and fifth grades. White non-Hispanic students represent 35 percent of the pre- kindergarten total,

TABLE 4.1
1991-1992 Profiles of the Three Schools

	Ashe 1991[a] K-5[b] before/after[c]	Porter 1990 PK-5 before/after	Pine Villa 1959 PK-5 after
Number of portables	0	0	25
Total student enrollment	841	982	1185
Assigned program capacity (no. of students)	927	926	664
Total number of 8 classroom teachers	35	42	60
Total number of teacher aides	1	2	20
Percentage of staff with masters degrees or higher	34	48	32
Total number of teachers in the $26,000-$29,000 range	17	17	19
Total number of teachers earning $42,000 and over	5	15	26

Source: Dade County Public Schools, *District and School Profiles, 1991-1992* (Miami: Dade County Public Schools, 1992).

[a] Date established
[b] Grade organization
[c] School care

however, and only 1 percent of the fifth grade total. Black non-His-panic students represent 51 percent of the pre-kindergarten total and 93 percent of the fifth grade total.[3] (see table 4.2)

Ashe and Porter were built to cope with the large growth of popu-lation in suburban Kendall. The selection of their principals, as well as

TABLE 4.2
Student Program Information

	White non-Hispanic		Black non-Hispanic		Hispanic		Asian and American Indian		
	Grade*	%	Grade	%	Grade	%	Grade	%	Total
Ashe									
K	37	27	11	8	91	65	—	—	159
1	50	33	9	6	91	59	3	2	153
2	47	31	13	8	92	60	2	1	154
3	35	23	7	5	105	70	3	2	150
4	33	25	5	4	92	70	1	1	131
5	27	24	7	6	79	69	1	1	114
TOTAL	229	27	52	6	550	65	10	1	841
Porter									
PK	9	45	1	5	9	45	1	5	20
K	63	39	10	6	79	48	11	7	163
1	64	36	12	7	91	51	10	6	177
2	64	39	14	8	80	48	7	4	165
3	62	34	12	6	104	56	7	4	185
4	65	40	13	8	77	47	8	5	163
5	36	33	9	8	58	53	6	6	109
TOTAL	363	37	71	7	498	51	50	5	982
Pine Villa									
PK	37	35	55	51	13	12	2	2	107
K	37	17	166	76	16	7	—	—	219
1	31	15	152	76	16	8	2	1	201
2	23	11	159	77	23	11	2	1	207
3	16	9	148	80	18	10	2	1	184
4	12	8	126	87	7	5	2	1	145
5	1	1	113	93	7	6	1	1	122
TOTAL	157	13	919	78	100	8	9	1	1,185

Source: Dade County Public Schools, *District and School Profiles, 1991-1992* (Miami: Dade County Public Schools, 1992).

*Grade refers to the number of students in each grade level.

their philosophies, were a direct outgrowth of a competition that was held to introduce innovative schools and programs into the Dade County Public School System. Both schools have heavily invested in the concept of shared decision making—modeled after the Japanese system of Total Quality Management. The name "Saturn School" is drawn directly from the General Motors Corporation model of Saturn car production in which there are "fewer union restrictions, new facilities, devoted workers hired by peers, labor integrated with management, new technology and management techniques with a new set of rules and standards."[4]

Both schools are strongly child-centered. Both have a remarkably similar instructional environment focusing on academic achievement and success. Each has focused on the development of literacy and skills in technology. Each emphasizes bilingual language acquisition in English and Spanish as well as science and mathematics achievement. Porter began in portable classrooms in 1990. Ashe opened a year later with a fully constructed building. Despite the fact that teachers and administrators talked about the difficulty of achieving academic goals in the 1992-93 hurricane school year, achievement and excellence within an orderly and well-disciplined environment were clear priorities.

The emphasis on academic excellence and the enthusiasm of teachers and administrators for the programs at Ashe and Porter was clearly communicated by Dr. Tarja Geis, one of Porter's two Saturn coordinators. She described Porter, "The School of Discovery," and its focus on science as a unifying instructional theme in the following way (note the use of terms such as "galley" for cafeteria, "mission control" for the central office, "discovery center" for library, and "galaxy" for grade group; all are part of the school's theme of space exploration and technology):

> We have the science lab for the intermediate grades and then we also have a science lab on wheels for the primary grades. The primary science teacher has a cart on wheels that she moves about the school. It's all hands on. Sometimes you'll see the children outside in the fields doing hands-on instruction, such as flying airplanes, and all sorts of fun activities for them. Last year we had an exploration lab the Exceptional Student Education (ESE) department put together based on NASA's exploration lab. ESE includes the gifted and learning disabled. They went to NASA, and toured their exploration lab, brought back ideas, and created one for the children here. Those children ran the lab. They were the teachers and the instructors. They did hands on activities and experiments. However, because the Chapter 1 office is using it, we haven't been able to use it this year. We hope to

have it again next year. . . . When we first started the plan for the school, the district science specialist helped us and gave us a lot of good ideas. We really wanted the theme of this school to be futuristic, a part of computers and technology and aerospace. We have two computer labs, one with Macintosh LCs, the sky lab upstairs, and one with IBMs donated after the hurricane. Our school is now totally networked to the Apple Lab, which means that any teacher in the classroom who has a computer can access the programs in the lab.[5]

Willie Kearney and Sheila Washington-Clark, second grade teachers at Porter, provided a second perspective on the school's mission. Sheila explained that the number of students from diverse language and cultural backgrounds had increased during the 1992-93 school year. According to her, Porter was basically composed of students who could easily be classified as minorities because of their cultural and linguistic backgrounds. She observed that with the students at Porter, although they were technically minorities, they did not necessary feel or act like the stereotype of a minority:

If you don't feel like a minority, are you a minority? I've noticed that the students [in this school] who are true minorities don't feel like minorities. I think that it's the way the teachers treat the students. At this school, we try to make the students' self-esteem be as high as possible.[6]

For Kearney, the school was a place where people learned about differences in a positive way:

When we find a student who is putting down another student, we can call the parents in and talk to them. We also talk to the students about it. We handle it by talking about race and ethnicity with the students. The students do not feel like minorities.[7]

Joanne Lasky, the assistant principal at Pine Villa, described her school as follows:

Pine Villa, the first Montessori school in Dade County, started in 1985-86. Melvin Denis is the third principal since the Montessori program opened at Pine Villa. The idea of the Montessori program is to promote integration. Montessori-type education had previously been available only through private schools for middle-class children. When the Montessori concept was implemented in Dade County, the ideas were found to be relevant for lower socioeconomic students too. Initially, there seemed to be discrepancies between the magnet Montessori and the already established

Pine Villa school. Magnet schools are not intended to include the whole school. They are intended to promote desegregation. Neighborhood children have the opportunity to participate in the Montessori program. But to establish a level of racial balance, the magnet programs must be kept at a thirty-seventy balance, meaning thirty percent of the local children and seventy percent of the children from outside the established school boundaries. Pine Villa has been sensitive to the needs and interests of the local community and has generally kept a forty-sixty balance so that more of the community children can attend.[8]

Lasky's comments suggest a certain amount of ambiguity concerning the Montessori program and its role in the community. For some, the Montessori program is a source of pride and represents an opportunity for people in the Pine Villa area. It is also a program that has been brought in from the outside and does not reflect educational traditions and practices of the local community.

Lasky elaborated on the perceptions of the community and the role of the school:

> Some of the people in the community have expressed concern about Pine Villa being a Montessori school that not everyone can attend. The community people may even say that they have been cheated because they see all of the equipment and the teachers in the Montessori classes, and not in the regular, non-magnet classrooms. Between $30,000 and $40,000 are required, depending on the grade level, to equip each Montessori classroom. In addition to all of the equipment, three adults are available in each Montessori class. However, Pine Villa is a Chapter 1 program throughout, so there are a great many more resources than there would be in a typical school. In addition, last year two Montessori classrooms were added, through Chapter 1, for the preschool students in the community. Chapter 1 has provided the computer lab and an additional resource teacher per grade to assist the teachers in curriculum development and instruction. There is no way that Pine Villa has been cheated. There are many resources here. If the Montessori program were to leave, the school would be just the same. Nothing has been taken away from the students because of the Montessori program. In fact, there are a great many benefits to having a magnet school. However, it is understandable that there would be some perceptions of inequality. Especially in times of stress, the notion of inequalities seems to reappear. (Lasky Interview)

Although not a member of the Pine Villa Community, Curtis Jenkins, the guidance counselor at Porter, provides an interesting description of the school and the local community. His perspective comes from having lived close to Pine Villa prior to the hurricane and having worked with the teachers and students there during the recovery process:

> The Pine Villa community is a working family community with public housing projects. There are people who are at a survival level, day-to-day, week-to-week, or month-to-month. That by itself is very stress producing. The more affluent are regular trades people and business people, who are also trying to make a go of a business. Not necessarily week-to-week, but always in the back of their mind trying to get it going, do it better. When we are talking about the importance of the school and its relative stability, the people have a grit and stick-to-itness, a drive to do what they need to do to get by, and to provide for their family. I think that for them, the rallying point is that school provides a place for their kids to be safe, to learn, to better themselves while they can concentrate on the other things that they need to concentrate on. There is a different type of participation, an infrequent participation in the school's life, because of time and the constraints of business and family. . . . The school is a point where the community can rally. The school then provides an important leadership role. [9]

Pine Villa is located approximately ten miles southeast of Porter. (see figure 4.1) Excepting the paired special education centers (Neva King Cooper and Ruth Owen Kruse), the distance between Pine Villa and G. L. Porter was as large as that between any of the ten paired schools in the county. Not only were the two schools geographically separated, but also they were culturally separated as well. The demographic profile of the students at Porter reflects racial, ethnic, and economic levels that are close to those of the county average. The children attending Pine Villa were overwhelming African-American and came from a significantly lower socioeconomic level.

Likewise the teachers from Pine Villa were largely African-American while the general population of teachers at Porter, like its students in general, paralleled the county's diverse ethnic and racial makeup. As observers, we were acutely aware of the cultural and social differences between the two schools. Nevertheless, the hurricane had made them one, and despite differences in race, socioeconomic class, and geographic location, they had the task of having to get on with the process of teaching and learning.

Many of the teachers at Porter—as did almost everyone living in the southern part of the county—had their own personal tragedies and preoccupations resulting from the hurricane. In general, however, they were not as hard hit by the storm as their colleagues from Pine Villa. Like their colleagues at Ashe, the teachers at Porter appeared to us to present a front of enthusiasm and positive affect—despite obvious stress and strain. In contrast, the teachers from Pine Villa appeared to be having a more difficult time coping with the after effects of the hurricane.

This perception was echoed by the teachers from Porter whom we heard make comments like "we have to work twice as hard, go the extra mile, to let the Pine Villa teachers know that we care— that we're glad to share our school with them." This theme of the need for sharing and supporting one another was echoed by a number of teachers and administrators at Porter. Despite the best of intentions, however, the reality was that the Pine Villa teachers not only had been devastated by the storm but also had been uprooted from their familiar environment and work site and thrust into a largely unknown setting.

All three schools, like the rest of the county, began classes on September 14, 1992—three weeks after the hurricane and two weeks late. The researchers' commitment to the schools and the larger school district was to conduct the hurricane study without intruding on the teachers' time or the instructional process. During the following months, we attended meetings, combed newspapers and other media sources, school system documents, and frequently visited the schools. With a few exceptions, we did not regularly interview teachers, however, until late in the spring 1993 semester, because we felt that to do so would seriously interfere with their work and inhibit the recovery process. We did interview administrators at both the school and district level; we used their insights to gain further understanding of the recovery process and how it was implemented.

REESTABLISHING NORMALCY

Probably no other single event marked the attempt to return to normalcy for the Dade County Community better than the opening of the schools on September 14, 1992. As Henry Fraind, Assistant Superintendent for District Office Management, Operations, and Communications explained:

> The first sign of normalcy is when the school bell rings. It was our desire and effort to make that bell ring in every school on September 14 all over the county.[10]

The notion that the opening of the schools would provide a return to the familiar was repeated by other administrators as well. For example, Rosemary Fuller, the Principal of Perrine Elementary School, explained how once the schools reopened people would begin to feel "Oh, the school's back, it's O.K. for us now."[11] Tarja Geis at Porter commented, after completing the first day of classes, that for many of the students "this is the only normalcy they've had since the hurricane."[12]

Teachers reported back to their schools on Thursday, September 10, 1992. Classes began the following Monday. All of the high schools in the county were able to open despite damage from the storm. A total of ten elementary and middle schools were so badly damaged in the hurricane that they could not reopen, even with emergency repairs. The schools were paired with relatively undamaged "home" schools located near the storm zone. Double sessions were set up in which the "home" school began its day at 7:15 A.M. and ended classes by 12:00 Noon; the "guest" school began its day at 12:30 P.M. and ended at 5:30 P.M.

Because the researchers had not yet gone through the normal university and school system review process in undertaking their research (this process was completed in November) and because it was crucial to begin to conduct observations and interviews in the schools as soon as possible, the decision was made to use Porter and Ashe as research sites. As "Saturn Schools" both had special research agreements with the university, thus making access less of a problem, and both principals readily agreed to our being guests in their schools.[13]

Both schools had survived the hurricane with relatively little damage. Each school had a south county location close to where the hurricane did the worst damage. Ashe was on a regular schedule. Porter was designated a "home" school with Pine Villa as its "guest"—Pine Villa having been severely damaged in the storm. We felt that Ashe and Porter would be particularly interesting to compare and contrast since they are located very near each other, are virtually identical in terms of their physical plants and design, and are both Saturn Schools. In particular, the fact that Porter was on double session with Pine Villa while Ashe was on a regular schedule provided opportunities for comparison.

THE TEACHERS RETURN TO
BOWMAN FOSTER ASHE

Our first experience in the schools following the hurricane took place at Ashe, where we observed the teachers return to school on Thursday, September 10, 1992. After a long, difficult drive through neighborhoods that had been heavily damaged by the storm, over ten miles of roads with only one or two traffic lights operating, we arrived at the school.

Although damage in the immediate neighborhood was quite extensive (many trees were down, and roofs had been blown off houses everywhere), the school showed relatively little damage from the storm. All of the building's windows were in place, and while there was visible evidence of the storm all around the grounds, the buildings seemed remarkably normal.

As the teachers began to assemble in the library, it seemed as though a normal school year was getting underway. As we watched closely, however, we realized that the teachers were more subdued than had been our experience in similar settings in previous years. They walked with each other in small groups through the hallways towards the library. People seemed to cluster together. In an effort to make light of the problems caused by the storm, the principal, Dr. Frazier Cheyney, wore a humorous T-shirt with a bold graphic proclaiming "I Survived Hurricane Andrew." He greeted each of the teachers as they came into the library.[14] Interestingly, in contrast to their principal, none of the teachers' clothing referred to the storm.

Once in the library, teachers gathered together in small clusters, talking almost in whispers. There was a lot of hugging and touching as they greeted each other. Quiet and concerned exchanges were made between them about their experiences after the storm. "How did you do?" "What happened to you and your family?" "Did you have much damage?" "Where were you during the storm?" And then the responses: "We're OK, but. . . ." As they shared their personal experiences of the storm, individual stories began to emerge. "So and so lost their house." "The electricity in my neighborhood only just came on yesterday." Or, "We still don't have any power. They say it may be a month." Despite descriptions of homes that were "blown out" and some even having to be bulldozed, the teachers kept on talking about being alright and even being lucky. There was evidence of remarkable courage and determination—a sense of people having survived and now needing to get on with their lives and their work with their students.

Despite a sense of a new beginning, there were important questions still left unanswered. "If we're still adjusting, ourselves, what will it be like for our students next week?" "How can we make plans for the whole year, when we can hardly think beyond the end of the day?"

The teachers were clearly wanting to say that things were OK and that they would get back to normal soon. Nevertheless, things clearly weren't OK. People's lives were anything but back to normal. The school's principal, for example, had lost most of his house. Yet, here he was, like many of the teachers, not even mentioning his personal loss, just getting back to work. "It's great to be alive, isn't it?" he said to the fifty or so teachers and staff assembled in the library. To which the group simply gave a loud round of applause.

The principal then explained that he had at first thought that they were going to be paired with another school, but sufficient repairs had been made so that double sessions would not be necessary. Cheers and applause immediately came again from the teachers who were clearly not only pleased for their colleagues, but also relieved at the idea of their lives not being further complicated by a double session schedule. The principal then said that if anyone had any special needs, he and his staff were there to help, but that he understood that "most of our needs are unspoken." After emphasizing that if people found themselves needing help in the weeks to come, it was important to let these needs be known, the principal then launched into a discussion of the parent evaluation of the school that had taken place at the end of the previous school year. He instinctively seemed to be emphasizing the positive and the upbeat: "The evaluations from the parents from last June were very good, and so on. . . ."

From then on, it was back to things as normal. The school year had begun. There was work to do, and everybody knew their job. The researchers were introduced along with the new teachers. A new training and research project from the university was discussed with the project's principal investigators outlining different aspects of the research. After the first hour, everyone took a break. After this, the teachers returned to work on curriculum plans and in-service training for the year. By the end of the morning, things appeared pretty much as they would have at the beginning of any normal school year. Before the teachers left for the day, a welcome back speech was broadcast to them by Octavio Visiedo, the Superintendent of Schools.

GILBERT L. PORTER AND PINE VILLA:
THE TEACHERS MEET

On Friday, September 11, 1992, the teachers from Pine Villa and Porter met for the first time. On Thursday, only the teachers from Porter reported to the Porter building in Kendall. The teachers from Pine Villa had returned to their school in Goulds and packed up their materials in preparation for the move to Porter. Coordinating the operation of two separate schools in one setting would be difficult enough under normal circumstances, but with the added complications caused by the hurricane it was even harder.

When the teachers from Pine Villa arrived and met their counterparts in Porter on Friday September 11, there were warm formal greetings and limited personal contact. Songs were sung and small gifts were exchanged between some of the teachers. There was very much of an attempt to unite the two staffs. The theme of sharing was emphasized by the Saturn school coordinator at Porter, Tarja Geis, who said: "We are truly blessed to have a school that we can share. We have a roof and walls and we have to do all that we can for the children and teachers who don't. It's hard right now. We're just still trying to pull ourselves together, but we have to do a lot more because we are here, and we have something that the others don't have. We have to share and we have to do it with a smile."

The formal greetings made by administrators and staff at Porter to the teachers from Pine Villa seemed to come from the heart. Perhaps the sincerity of the Porter response was a result of having shared the experience of the hurricane with their Pine Villa colleagues. In many respects, the hurricane was democratic. It cut across all of the neighborhoods and people and all of the ethnicities and diverse language groups in the southern half of the county. The teachers from Porter had suffered along with their less fortunate colleagues at Pine Villa—perhaps not as badly but certainly in ways that gave them insight into the suffering of their Pine Villa counterparts.

THE FIRST DAY OF SCHOOL AT
GILBERT L. PORTER AND PINE VILLA

Porter students and teachers were assigned the first session. Pine Villa would attend in the afternoon. Most of the children coming to Porter came with their parents or arrived in private minibuses. Many of the parents were taking still photographs and making videos of this first day of school.

Porter borders the edge of the Everglades on its western side. On the eastern edge of the school is a brand new housing development. At first, things appeared relatively normal, but as the sun began to rise we could see the broken roof tiles, the blown out windows, and the tattered shreds that were once stately coconut palms. The owners of these houses, despite the destruction, were lucky. Many were still at least partially habitable and by now had running water. A light rain began to fall as the students poured into the school.

Many of the children appeared to be tired and frightened. Teachers, volunteer parents, and administrators were highly visible in welcoming the children and their families as they arrived at school. A two-piece musical combo made up of two teachers played a series of songs to greet the children. The combo featured the theme song from the musical *Annie*, with lyrics about a brighter day tomorrow, and the school's theme song.

The theme of welcome echoed throughout the whole school. It was expressed in the voices of the combo stationed at the front of the school, on the faces of the teachers and administrators located throughout the building and the grounds, and on the faces of the parent volunteers who were part of the welcoming process. Most importantly, it also began to show itself on the faces of the children as they entered the school and became involved in the process of starting again.

One could not help but sense that the school was an island in a difficult sea of confusion and turmoil. Here was a place that not only was welcoming but also was familiar, a place which promised the hope of normalcy and the return to what life had been like before the storm. It was this theme, that of the school reestablishing a sense of community, that we sensed so strongly that day. Here was not only a new beginning but also a connection to the past and a link to the future.

Porter operates around a theme that focuses on space exploration. The school's colors are red, white, and blue. Its office is referred to as "mission control," and the school's curriculum is organized around activities related to space exploration and science. Students, teachers, and parent volunteers were often dressed in T-shirts and jump suits reflecting the school's space exploration theme.

Even though this was only the school's second year of operation, we sensed that there were already traditions emerging that gave the school and its students and teachers a sense of identity. The space theme created an ethos of unity and excitement despite the problems caused by the hurricane and its aftermath. We suspected that the school colors and their obvious connection to patriotic themes were important as well. In driving through shattered neighborhoods as part of relief efforts in the days immediately following the hurricane, we were constantly impressed by the number of American flags that were being flown over destroyed homes and businesses. One sensed that survival, of making it through the storm and of starting over, was somehow closely associated in many people's minds with feelings of patriotism and country.

Students were registered, their attendance noted, and then they were sent on to their classrooms. During the first two weeks of school, students in both home schools and guest schools received free lunches. The importance of the school as a social center and support agency became particularly clear as the Pine Villa students arrived in the early afternoon. Long lines snaked out from the cafeteria as students lined up to receive a hot meal.

Children in the morning session had supplies set out for them. On a table outside of the cafeteria students could get shrink-wrapped packages of school supplies—different ones for each grade level. It was clear that careful thought had been given by the school to seeing that children who were without adequate supplies of their own would start the school year without any difficulty.

During the morning session parent volunteers talked about how difficult it was to get things back to normal. One mother explained, for example, how:

> Every time we get power in this community we have another lightning storm that blows out the transformers. The power continues to fluctuate and knocks out the appliances. Parents are still distracted, trying to keep up with the basics. I've had a hard time myself. It wasn't until Saturday that I realized that my own children didn't have any clothes to wear to school. Some of the parents got together the supplies that the children would need such as tablets and pencils and paper and organized them for different grade levels. And we've taken up a collection for the children who couldn't afford supplies.

The principal and teachers emphasized that there would be no formal textbook instruction during the first few days of school. Instead, children would talk about their experiences during the hurricane and perhaps write about or draw pictures of what they had gone through. In the fifth grade class, the teacher asked her students questions such as "What do you suppose animals do in a hurricane?" or "Have you heard about any of Florida's endangered animals since the storm, such as the Florida panther?" Each teacher was free to choose what he or she thought was important to do. It was clear as the school day progressed that the first day would emphasize thoughtful discussion, being together, and understanding what the children and the community had experienced.

One of the researchers was informally included in a fourth grade class. The assigned teacher heading up the class used cut-outs of hurricane symbols which she gave to each child. The children drew pictures of their experiences on these symbols and then gathered on the floor in a circle to share their stories. Some of the children used highly animated language as they told stories about their experience. One child described the sliding glass door that bowed back and forth in the wind and finally shattered, sending shards of glass over the living room floor. Another child spoke about spending the night of the storm in his grandfather's bathroom huddled with seven other family members while the house shook around them and the roof was blown away. Some of the children who were more proficient in Spanish than in English talked about their experiences in Spanish. This bilingual communication posed no problem for the teacher, the researcher, and most of the other students, who were also proficient in both languages.

Many of the students described listening to Spanish television and radio during the hurricane. One of the children indicated that both during and after the storm his family had problems because so much of the emergency information was only available in English and his family—especially his mother—had difficulty with the language.

After talking about the hurricane, the children returned to the large tables that were used instead of desks in the classroom. Four to six students sat at each table to do a word association game. She explained that they were to write down a word that they associated with each word she said. The first word she said was "hurricane"; then she said "hurricane" nine more times. Each time the teacher said "hurricane," the students wrote down another word which they associated with it. Afterwards she asked them to develop group definitions of the term using the words that they had written down. One child, for example, wrote associations like hurricane = tornado, = earthquake, = wind, = breeze, = tail, = eye, = water, = thunder, = lightning, = storm. Illustrated at the top of the paper were two drawings of what appear to be horned devils along with a traffic light whose border surrounded the word association list. A second student listed the following words: hurricane = destroy, = wind, = storms, = car, = damage, = scared, = strong, = break down, = slow, and = bad. While this student did not include a drawing, he wrote at the top of his paper that "a hurricane is something that destroys apartments, cars, houses and other stuff."

Group definitions were developed by the students at each table in the classroom. These included: "A hurricane is a strong storm that brings a lot of wind and water." "A hurricane is a storm with winds over seventy-five miles per hour that can do a lot of damage. Hurricanes range from category 1 to 5, Hurricane Andrew was a category 5. Andrew cost twenty billion dollars in damage. The eye of the hurricane is quiet. Hurricanes are the worst natural disasters."

Having completed group definitions, the children went to lunch and then took a walk around the school during which they were instructed to observe the damage that had occurred to the school so that they could later document this information in drawings and writings.

The school day ended for the children at Porter just after noon. The day had gone well, without major incidents. However, as the Porter children were being dismissed, the children from Pine Villa began arriving. Gridlock ensued. While tempers remained calm, the process of leaving and arriving was chaotic.

PINE VILLA ARRIVES

About 12:20 buses began to roll in from Pine Villa. Among the very first was one driven by a regular bus driver with a banner draped across the front grill proclaiming: "Thank you G.L. Porter. We love you from Pine Villa." A long stream of buses, driven by military personnel, followed. Police were directing the traffic in front of the school.

The children and the teachers in the morning session were a mix of Latino and North American ethnicities and cultures. The rhythms of Spanish and English were heard throughout the school as the children from the morning session departed for their homes. The afternoon students, few of whom were accompanied by their parents, were almost all African-American. Their eyes were bright, but their faces were silent.

The teacher combo again sang songs of welcome as the Pine Villa children arrived. This time the teachers and children from Porter joined them in dancing and displaying banners of welcome to the new arrivals. Despite the music and dancing, most of the children from Pine Villa kept their faces down and only occasion ally looked up to see the festivities. A song of welcome had been specially composed for the Pine Villa students. Just simple chords, it repeated over and over again the important message that the Pine Villa students were welcome in their temporary new school. The song seemed to reach out with invisible fingers and touch the newly arrived students. As the Pine Villa children heard the name of their school being sung, an occasional smile and tentative wave of the hand could be seen.

The ethos of the school quickly changed as the families and the students on private buses, bikes, and on foot from the morning session left the campus, their places taken by the quiet, somber displaced children from Pine Villa. Their school year was beginning in a strange neighborhood, in a new school, after a long journey by bus. Conscious of imposing on the newly arrived students and teachers from Pine Villa, we left. In walking away, the words that the morning teachers had spoken echoed in the silence: "We have to reach out. We have to let them know that we care—that we're here for them too. They are a part of our school, and we have to help them through this crisis."

SCHOOL THEMES AS PART OF THE REBUILDING PROCESS

A school is, or can be, much more than a building in which students and teachers live for part of a day, five days a week. Schools can be powerful places, magical places, places where minds come together and thoughts are shared. When a community has shared a tragedy, such as a hurricane, schools can be important places for many reasons. Throughout the process of observing the opening of the schools, we became aware of certain themes that created the school atmosphere. Here we discuss some of these themes as they seemed to be apparent on the first day back at Porter and Pine Villa.

It was clear that at Porter, on the first day, a sense of community was being established. For example, parents acted as volunteers assisting the teachers and administrators in welcoming the children and families, accompanying them to registration in the library and then on to their classrooms.

It was clear that the community was uniting with the school. Friendly welcomes were heard throughout the morning. These welcomes could be observed everywhere, not only in the voices of the teachers singing but also on the faces of the adults located throughout the building and grounds. Most importantly, the welcoming feeling also began to show itself on the faces of the children as they entered the school and began the process of starting again, of learning about what happened to their friends, and of seeing that at least somewhere, there was some normalcy in the world.

Porter is an interesting school to observe. From the outside it looks like many other new schools in south Florida. Nevertheless, Porter has a distinctive flavor, even with its marquee destroyed. The building and the people in it communicate positive expectations and a sense of idealism. The school refers to itself as GLP/SLD—Gilbert L. Porter, the school of discovery. The school theme of space exploration is reflected in the school colors: red, white, and blue. The students, teachers, administrators, and parent volunteers dressed in clothing ranging from tailored suits and jumpsuits to T-shirts with the school colors and logo. On the first day of school, many people were dressed in the Porter colors. Seeing the red, white, and blue raised a sense of patriotism and a spirit of solidarity among many who joined in the official first day back. The colors and the theme also gave the students and teachers a sense of identity and unity after the storm.

The school colors and their obvious connection to a sense of patriotism were important for an additional reason as well. In the days following the hurricane U.S. flags were often flown over destroyed homes and businesses. One sensed that the survival from the storm and the beginning to rebuild afterwards were somehow closely associated with the sense of patriotism and community felt by many South Floridians. The students and teachers of Porter, perhaps unintentionally, echoed the sentiments of the community as they dawned their clothes for the first day of school.

During the first two weeks of school both the Porter and Pine Villa students, like students throughout the hurricane damaged area, received free lunches. The importance of the school as a social center and support agency was particularly clear during this period of the recovery process. Long lines snaked out of the cafeteria as students entered to receive a hot meal. For many it was the only hot meal they would receive since the electricity was not on in many areas, and neither grocery stores or restaurants had not yet opened for business.

The children could purchase shrink-wrapped packages of school supplies, including textbooks for each grade level, pencils, and paper. Parent volunteers had been quick to organize the materials for the children whose families might not have been able to go shopping for school supplies. The care with which these materials were organized was another clear reflection of the desire to start school off well and to ensure that students had all that they needed to begin work.

THE PARENT MEETING AT G. L. PORTER

Although both Pine Villa and Porter were sharing facilities together well, there was concern by the Porter parents about their children having to attend school on double session. On September 23, 1992, an evening parent meeting was held at the school to talk to parents about the post-Hurricane Andrew arrangements.

Frederic Zerlin, Porter's principal, began the meeting by saying:

> Many of you, like many of the staff, have lost their homes. Many of you have had to wait for insurance adjusters and other things. We all have these problems. But most importantly, we have our school, our home within this community. On August 24 after the hurricane, I was driving around and I came out to the Hammocks [the neighborhood in which the school is located], and I could not believe the extent of the damage. . . . I was shaking when I got up to the school. I noticed that the marquee was blown away. Then I noticed the trees were damaged. But I couldn't tell about the school because the roof is flat, so I didn't know what was inside. I went inside and found very minor damage. The main air conditioner had problems, and some of the classrooms had been soaked. All curable. No structural damage. Everything, as far as structure, was fine. Monday was the hurricane, Thursday was the principals' meeting where Mr. Visiedo met with all the Region six principals and said: "Many of the schools in the south area, Region six, are devastated. There is no way they can open on time. Those of you in schools that weren't too badly damaged, are you willing accept another school?" Now I was truly thankful that there was a halo around our school. I truly feel that what we are doing now is going to pay off in the end. It's going to bring a lot of good for us at Porter and for the community. I said to Mr. Visiedo, "I have no problem opening my arms to another school."[15]

Zerlin explained to the parents how:

> Pine Villa not only was damaged by Hurricane Andrew but also looted. They had more damage from the looting than from the hurricane. . . . Your support is greatly appreciated. We have opened our hearts to Pine Villa Elementary. Pine Villa is down U.S. 1 in Goulds. Their school is absolutely devastated. Mr. Denis, the principal, is having a meeting tomorrow with the architects. They are trying to patch the school right now. . . . How long is Pine Villa going to be here? We don't have a good answer. However, we are making the best of what we have got.[16]

Zerlin went on to thank the faculty and staff for having "made the opening of the school successful." Asking them to stand, he said, "Let's give the staff at GLP a big hand." Zerlin concluded by saying, "And I just want to say to you—my community—I love you."

Tarja Geis, also addressed the parents and teachers attending the meeting:

> When we think about the possibilities, we realize that we are very fortunate. We are very fortunate to be in a position to have a wonderful, safe, nice school. . . .[17]

Naomi Davis, the school's other Saturn coordinator, talked about how established procedures had to be revamped because of the additional students using the school's "galley" (This involved students having to carry their "space" or cafeteria trays back from the galley to their classrooms in order to eat) and how aftercare and before care programs would be available to help parents cope with their children following the hurricane.

The meeting concluded with "galaxy" coordinators (grade level chairs or heads) explaining to the parents the curriculum for Porter's double session, which now ran from 7:15 to 12:15. Joe Jackson, the county's supervisor for psychological services, provided suggestions for helping parents work with children who were still upset by the storm.

CONCLUSION

The opening of school after Hurricane Andrew provided many opportunities to observe the relationship between the community and the school and to examine some of the roles that the schools played in the rebuilding process. During this time we noted several important themes illustrating these roles. Focusing specifically on the interactions and behaviors that occurred within the three target schools during the opening days of the school year, four themes emerged: (a) the importance of the schools in reestablishing a sense of community, (b) the unique role played by individual schools serving as focal points around which the community could unite, (c) the role of the schools in creating a sense of identity for the students and faculty, and (d) the role of the schools as social and medical support centers.

Each of these themes represents an important contribution beyond the schools' traditional role of providing instructional services. These themes represent important factors in the rebuilding process, ones which were powerful resources in reestablishing normalcy. As we observed Ashe, Porter, and Pine Villa during the remainder of the school year, we saw these same themes, and others, work together to promote many positive experiences for the students and families, as well as faculty and staff.

After the school year had begun, we closed the doors on the classrooms and began to observe the rebuilding process from the hallways, offices, and special events hosted by the schools. We learned about the rebuilding through interactions with administrators, teachers, and parents. These findings are presented in subsequent chapters.

NOTES

1. Interview with Joe Jackson, conducted by Sandra H. Fradd and Eugene F. Provenzo, Jr., March 1, 1993, Miami, Florida.

2. Dade County Public Schools, *District and School Profiles, 1991-1992* (Miami: Dade County Public Schools, 1992).

3. Ibid.

4. Tarja Geis and Frederic Zerlin, *Saturn School Project*, October 27, 1989, p. 80. Internal school document.

5. Interview with Tarja Geis conducted by Sandra H. Fradd, May 1993, Miami, Florida.

6. Interview with Sheila Washington-Clark conducted by Sandra Fradd, May 1993, Miami, Florida.

7. Interview with Willie Kearney conducted by Sandra H. Fradd, May 1993, Miami, Florida.

8. Interview with Joanne Lasky conducted by Sandra H. Fradd and Eugene F. Provenzo, Jr., May 1993, Miami, Florida. The following quote is from the Lasky interview and cited in the text.

9. Interview with Cutis Jenkins conducted by Sandra H. Fradd, May 1993, Miami, Florida.

10. Interview with Sally Osborne, Nelson Diaz, Henry Fraind, and Jerry Salcines conducted by Sandra H. Fradd and Eugene F. Provenzo, Jr., Miami, Florida, December 16, 1992.

11. Pitsch, Mark, "Down But Not Out, Patched Dade Schools Open," *Education Week*, 12, no. 3 (September 1992): p. 1.

12. Laurie, Goldstein, "School Routine Soothes Andrew's Trauma," *Washington Post*, September 16, 1992, p. 4A.

13. Under the Saturn School program, administrators, together with faculty and staff, submitted proposals to develop innovative educational programs. Competitions were conducted, and winners were selected based on outstanding program design. New programs were developed and staff were hired while the schools' physical plants were being constructed. This was done under the leadership of the school's principal and in collaboration with a Saturn school coordinator, select staff, and various members of the community. Three Saturn schools set up programs for research and collaboration with the School of Education at the University of Miami. These included South Pointe Elementary School, Gilbert L. Porter, and Bowman Ashe.

14. A large T-Shirt business developed after the hurricane with vendors located along main highways throughout Dade County. Interestingly, while newspaper accounts indicated that there were sales for these T-Shirts, they were rarely seen in the community.

15. Frederic Zerlin speaking at the September 23, 1992, parent meeting for Gilbert L. Porter Elementary School.

16. Ibid.

17. Tarja Geis speaking at the September 23, 1992, parent meeting for Gilbert L. Porter Elementary School.

5

The Ongoing Rebuilding Process

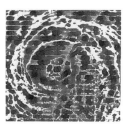

Ashe, Pine Villa, and Porter were only three of the many South Dade schools that were affected by the hurricane. Throughout the entire school district—including those areas that were not physically affected by Hurricane Andrew—the normal flow of the school year was unavoidably redefined as a result of the storm.

This chapter provides an overview of the difficulties faced by the public school system in the weeks and months following the hurricane. This information included in this chapter suggests that the problems faced by the three schools we studied were neither unique nor the worst possible situations faced by educators, students, and local communities.

COPING AND LEARNING TO SHARE

Besides the two week delay in opening the schools, student enrollments were significantly affected by the hurricane. On the first day of school, September 14, 1992, 250,100 students came to class. Enrollment had increased to 267,324 students by the following Wednesday—but this must be compared to the 312,000 students who were enrolled throughout the system during the previous year.[1]

There were a variety of reasons for decreased enrollment. Many students had left Dade, moving north with their families to Broward and Palm Beach Counties, while others were sent out of state. Others did not attend school because of a lack of transportation or because they did not have any clothes to wear for school.

Emergency services and aid from outside the hurricane zone gradually helped improve the situation. For example, the Nike Shoe Company donated 2,000 pairs of running shoes that were distributed by the

United Teachers of Dade to children in need of footwear. The Sears Corporation contributed hundreds of thousands of dollars in clothing for children. These contributions were particularly important since much of the used clothing donated from around the country was not useable. In addition to contributions made by large corporations, local churches, as well as civic and professional groups such as the Kiwanis and AHEAD (American Hispanic Educators Association of Dade), provided funds and clothing for children at specific schools.

As the months progressed, the process of rebuilding proved to be long and tiring. The following section provides a brief overview of some of the difficulties faced by the schools. Caribbean Elementary School, for example, had been so extensively damaged that it had to be leveled and completely rebuilt. Initial estimates were that portable classrooms could be set up on the school site while a totally new building was constructed. The plan was for the children to be able to return to the school by early January 1993 so that they would not have to continue double sessions with South Miami Heights Elementary School. By January portables were still not in place.[2] Instead, fifteen portables were sent to South Miami Heights Elementary School. Estimates placed the completion of the new school as being at least eighteen months away.[3]

Like Caribbean Elementary School, R. R. Moton Elementary was devastated by the storm. A fine arts magnet and neighborhood school for fifth and sixth graders located in West Perrine, the school was paired after the storm with Blue Lakes Elementary School, eight miles north. Moton's 450 students, including 250 from the dance, drama, music, and visual arts magnets, were housed in seven portables at Blue Lakes Elementary.[4]

Moton was scheduled to move back to fourteen portables in West Perrine during the 1993-94 school year. Estimates indicated that it would take three years to complete the new building, which would have a projected enrollment of 885 students. As was the case with Caribbean, the rebuilding of Moton was seen as the driving force in reestablishing the West Perrine area.[5]

At Perrine Elementary School complaints were heard by the beginning of October that the school had been opened prematurely. Problems arose concerning mold, warped furniture, damaged ceiling tiles, and water-soaked books. Maintenance workers, staff, and parents spent weekdays and weekends cleaning and repairing the facility. Special reconstruction help for the school was provided by units from the U.S. Navy.[6]

The students at Redland Elementary School were first on double session at Avocado Elementary and later at Air Base Elementary. With the loss of Homestead Air Force Base, as well as the devastation in the community, most of the students attending the school moved elsewhere, reducing its enrollment from 1,080 students prior to the hurricane to approximately 200 after the storm. At first, Air Base shared its facilities with Chapman Elementary School. Once Chapman moved, the "Redland Wanderers" moved into the school, thus relieving overcrowded conditions at Avocado. Many of the children attending Redland will probably never attend the actual Redland physical plant.[7]

For some schools, the process of rebuilding was particularly difficult because of extraordinary circumstances. Air Base Elementary— which in 1959 was one the first public schools to be desegregated in the state of Florida—found itself not only seriously damaged but also devoid of nearly all of its students. The loss of Homestead Air Base, combined with the departure of thousands of civilians from the Homestead area, left the school with less than one fifth of its previous student population.

TEACHERS AND THE CRISIS

Teachers played a vital role in reestablishing normalcy in the schools and in the lives of the children they taught. Although large numbers of them had suffered catastrophic damage to their own homes, they were expected to create stable environments for the children with whom they worked. In the weeks and months immediately following the storm, many teachers expressed the feeling that returning to their classrooms and worrying about the needs of their students provided a way to escape their own worries. Glady Mickens, a teacher at Air Base Elementary School, for example, explained how coming to school "takes me away from the environment I'm currently in. I know I've got air-conditioning here, light. And then I'm going to see the kids."[8] Helping their students and escaping their own problems was a welcome relief for many of the teachers. Carolyn Trentler, another teacher at Air Base Elementary, explained how working at her job provided relief from the stress imposed by the hurricane: "when you have someone who needs your help and your attention . . . I slip right into it without giving a thought to the other things. It's like going to a movie. It's an escape."[9]

In the three schools where we conducted observations and interviews, the administrators and teachers put forward a remarkable effort to
bring things back to normal. In fact, many were coping with major
problems as a result of the hurricane. Shirley Hartley, the music teacher
at Pine Villa, for example, missed the first few months of school as a
result of losing her home in Cutler Ridge. After she returned to teach at
the school, she consistently presented an upbeat and enthusiastic image
to her students. As her principal Melvin Denis described her:

> She's a bundle of energy. There's nothing she wouldn't do for the kids.
> Because her job requires her to move around, she's learned to work well
> with everyone around her. It helps that there was always a smile on her
> face.[10]

Despite being on temporary leave, Hartley explained her feelings in the
following way: "I didn't like being away, I visited the school about
once a week. Coming back to work felt great." Hartley's return to school
in the fall not only was important to her, but also was a reason for cele-
bration among the school's children. Laykesha Mills, an eleven year-old
in the fifth grade, explained: "We missed her. When she got back we
were hugging her and kissing her."[11]

Hartley felt that her school was a place where she could make a
difference by helping students feel like they had a place where they
belonged. Her efforts were by no means confined to just teaching music.
Reestablishing the 160 member girl scout troop that she had begun ten
years before was also equally important to the process of recovering
from the hurricane.[12]

The process of returning to normalcy was neither swift nor auto-
matic for many of the teachers. Just how devastating the hurricane was
can be seen in the personal accounts of many of the teachers whom we
interviewed. Faye McCloud, for example, whose account of the storm
was presented in Chapter 1, explained how the experience of the storm
had almost totally consumed her energy and spirit—even seven months
later. Rebuilding was a tedious and difficult process:

> Here we are, seven months later, and we are still suffering. We had been in
> our home three years and one month. We had taken our time furnishing it
> and we had loved it so—all the emotional attachment. We know that the
> physical items can be replaced, not the mementos and the pictures, but
> the physical things, can be replaced. But to have lost it all in a period of
> four hours, it was just incredible.[13]

After the storm McCloud lived in seven different places. During the first week, for example, she lived with her mother whose house in Richmond Heights had also been seriously damaged. Often, just to get some privacy, she and her family would sit in their car in the driveway. For McCloud it was a period of tension and stress—one in which the future was by no means clear:

> I didn't know how I could deal with my job and its demands. I remember that I was grateful that school didn't open for several weeks. I remember that we drove by the school and it looked that nothing much had happened to it. I could see that there had been roof damage and the trees were destroyed, but it didn't look like the massive destruction that took place in my area. (McCloud Interview)

Actually, returning to school was a powerful emotional experience for McCloud: "I remember coming back to school that first day. I remember being overwhelmed by the whole event." Coming back made her once again relive the storm. As she explained:

> I had a hard time coming back. I remember thinking that I really believed in my heart that we were not going to make it thought the hurricane. It did not occur to me that I would live. I felt that we were going to die. I really, really thought we were going to die. It was such a horrible feeling, the feeling of helplessness. I remember thinking that it is such a shame for us to have to leave this earth. (McCloud Interview)

Coming back to work at the school, however, was critical to McCloud's personal recovery from the storm. Talking with her colleagues and friends, she found others who had gone through experiences similar to her own—people who could understand and share her feelings of personal loss and the trauma caused by the storm for both herself and her family. As she recalled:

> I remember coming to work that first day and everyone was so sensitive. I remember that we talked about pulling together. It was so good and reassuring to hear this from people who understood. I thought that maybe I'd be the only one, that maybe people wouldn't understand. Everyone was very sensitive and supportive. So many others had gone though the very same thing. When you have experienced what we experienced in the hurricane, it really turns around your whole value system—your priorities, everything. You think, "We're here; we're here on this earth. Thank God! We're alive to reach out to each other—to start being human." (McCloud Interview)

For McCloud, Hurricane Andrew provided a means of connecting not only with her colleagues in new ways, but also with her neighbors—many of whom she had barely known before the storm.

> To me, one lesson that I saw, and I think that a lot of people experienced, was the privacy fence. You very well might not know your neighbors. When those fences came down, we had to deal with each other—to share with each other. "You have water, and I need some. Can I have some of your water?" (McCloud Interview)

For McCloud, there was the realization of how fragile life could be. At the same time, there was an appreciation of the basic and most elemental things that life offers. Long waiting lines, which had become common, were suddenly acceptable. As she explained, she developed a new set of priorities—an ordering of what was important and unimportant. She found herself suddenly grateful to

> get a mouthful of food. You might think that you would never eat something, but when the truck comes around and brings it to you, it doesn't matter. You are grateful. If I had to glean any good from this hurricane experience, it would be that bottom line. We're all vulnerable. Anything that we have can be taken away. That is the message I get from this experience. (McCloud Interview)

For McCloud, the trauma caused by the storm was not one that would readily go away. Seven months later, she explained: "I still feel the pain. Not just about Faye and her personal losses and vulnerability. I feel that it's a loss for everyone." (McCloud Interview)

Yet, even in the pain and trauma of the hurricane's aftermath, new possibilities and educational models emerged. Among the most widely discussed was the school system's Project Phoenix.

PROJECT PHOENIX

The rebuilding effort of the school system was inevitably part of a larger political process. Local educational leaders and university researchers realized that the hurricane provided a series of opportunities as well as a set of obstacles to be overcome. Project Phoenix was implemented in the first few weeks after the hurricane as an effort to rebuild the schools and the community. The idea for Project Phoenix was a direct result of a phone call made four days after the storm by then Secretary of Education, Lamar Alexander, to Superintendent Visiedo. Alexander suggested that funds would be made available from the U. S. Department of Education for rebuilding the schools provided that the school system created an innovative program for rebuilding the schools that would meet the educational needs of the Twenty-first Century. Using the hurricane as an opportunity to undertake a new direction for the schools, the school system described Phoenix as being responsible for "rebuilding and revitalizing the schools damaged or destroyed by Hurricane Andrew." (McCloud Interview, p. 3) According to the school system, Phoenix was intended to

> catalyze the essential elements of educational change through participation in school-based decision-making models. These schools will search for ways to solve the many educational, psychological, and social problems that students and their families are experiencing. (McCloud Interview)

Project Phoenix was formally presented to the school board by Deputy Superintendent Phyllis L. Cohen and Pat Tornillo, the Executive Director of the United Teachers of Dade, at the October 14, 1993 special hurricane conference session. The program was, in fact, a means by which current reforms already underway in the school system could be expanded and further implemented. These reforms included the following:

1. the establishment of competency-based curriculum standards which would result in improved student achievement within a two to three year period;

2. the implementation of research-based models drawn from local and national sources. These would include, but not be limited to the Comer School Project, the Accelerated Schools Project, Success for All and the CORE Knowledge Program;

3. setting up prototype school models emphasizing outreach programs for intervention and prevention and increased parental involvement;

4. establishing school choice programs developed collaboratively by parents, teachers and administrators; and

5. improving alternative programs by developing satellite programs that would meet the unique needs of at-risk students.[14]

According to Cohen, Project Phoenix would bring about "a renaissance in urban education," one which would provide a model for the rest of the nation and a means by which "to draw population back to South Dade; a way to hasten the recovery phase; and a way to create a microcosm of a model urban school system."[15]

Among the most interesting details of the Project Phoenix proposal was the establishment of full-service schools, outreach and daycare centers, and adult literacy centers. In this context, the impact of the hurricane on the school system is extremely interesting. Rather like the destruction of the industrial base in Germany and Japan as a result of the Second World War, the destruction of much of the school system in the southern half of the county was being used as an exceptional opportunity to redefine the system and to implement new and important innovations.

The extent to which Project Phoenix was intended to implement reforms already underway in the school system can be seen in comments by Pat Tornillo, the head of the teachers union:

> The support and development of educational reform has been a major priority of the United Teachers of Dade, this school board, and the superintendent for many years now. As a leading partner in the growth of site-based decision making, it is with a great deal of anticipation that we embark with the school board and the superintendent on Project Phoenix. . . . Project Phoenix will rebuild the educational life of each community. . . . The application of the shared decision-making principal to the implementation of this project, is a natural step in the evolution of that process. But what's different about it? What's different is that Project Phoenix stresses curriculum changes. Shared decision-making will take a quantum leap from process in many instances, to focusing on the delivery of improved instruction to students and the enhancement of student achievement. That has always been our goal. We have the opportunity to do that in Project Phoenix.[16]

Schools in Regions five and six, as part of the Phoenix program, would become theme schools. As Associate Superintendent Nelson Diaz explained,

> The entire community, including parents, the teachers, the principals, the custodians—everybody—would get together and decide what kind of schools they want.[17]

Theme schools would serve the needs of the community and promote educational innovation. One of the elementary through secondary school "feeder patterns" (elementary, middle school, and high school geographic clusters) in the storm affected area had already decided that it would emphasize agricultural training as its unifying theme. According to Diaz, the theme schools that would be set in place as part of Project Phoenix would act as a means by which to help "draw the community together and to encourage families that had moved away from the southern part of the district to move back." (ODFS Interview)

By mid-November, the Dade County Public Schools had received $12.5 million from the federal government to undertake the first stages of Project Phoenix. These funds were provided with the understanding that the state of Florida would match the federal contribution. Additional funding of up to $10 million from the federal government was anticipated by the school system.

School system officials voiced their concern in interviews in December of 1992 that the new Clinton administration might affect plans for Project Phoenix. Funding for the project was at least loosely tied in with the America 2000 program, a part of the school reform effort of the Bush administration. The demands placed on the school system as a result of the hurricane became merged with national political agendas and national efforts at educational reform.

In undertaking the rebuilding of the school system after Hurricane Andrew, there was a strong need to maintain a balanced perspective that considered the needs of the entire county and its schools. As Superintendent Visiedo said at the Board's special conference session on October 14:

> The most difficult thing that we are doing throughout the whole operation is maintaining a balanced perspective on the needs of the entire school district—not just a particular region. We cannot forget the fact that there are schools in regions one through four that have been affected, and that every child is a victim. There may be some who were not directly affected by the hurricane, in that they might not have lost their homes or might not have had to move out of their schools; however, they have been affected by the extreme overcrowding of their classes. Additionally, the students in the receiving schools may have additional stress, or teachers who live in Regions five and six are working in regions one through four. (ODFS Interview, Conference Session, p. 12)

Visiedo viewed the entire district, not just the south end of the county, as being affected by the hurricane. Transfers of students out of schools in the southern part of the county to schools in its northern end proved to be enormously disruptive. Facilities and resources had already been strained. The addition of many new students to the district's northern schools increased the strain on both resources and faculty at these sites. The superintendent's concern was that the district, in its entirety, had to recover as quickly as possible. To speed the recovery process, Project Phoenix provided a rallying point.

TEACHERS RESPOND TO DISTRICT DEMANDS

While the community responded well to programs such as Project Phoenix, many teachers throughout the district found themselves placed under additional pressure due to storm recovery efforts. In our discussions with teachers, and in our observations of them in the three schools where our research was primarily focused, we developed an appreciation for the extraordinary efforts that were being made to create a normal environment for children. This was done while these individuals were coping with major personal problems involved in rebuilding their lives after the storm.

Teachers faced a particularly difficult challenge—providing as normal a setting as possible for students while managing their own lives. In September, just a few weeks after the storm, South Dade teachers together with Dade administrators confronted Governor Lawton Chiles about the difficulties of meeting personal needs while continuing to help children and the community cope with the crisis. Edith Parker, a Florida City Elementary School teacher, for example, told the governor that teachers like herself were "walking on an emotional tightrope." Roger Frese, a regional superintendent, emphasized that "I don't want people to see that the school's open and think everything is OK."[18]

It was estimated that, as the building process continued, more and more families would return to the South Dade area. Teachers would be needed to maintain the quality of the school program. District administrators also lobbied Governor Chiles for more money to rebuild the damaged schools and to keep teachers who might be released from their jobs because of the reduction in the number of students. While officials expected insurance and federal assistance to cover most costs resulting from the storm damage, they also emphasized the need for state support in the recovery process.[19]

As the school year progressed, it became increasingly evident that teachers were under severe stress resulting not only from the rebuilding process but also from the new initiatives that were being proposed by federal, state, and local officials. In March 1993, teachers throughout the county voted overwhelmingly to postpone new school programs, such as Blueprint 2000 and Project Phoenix. According to Pat Tornillo, the Executive Director and lead negotiator for the United Teachers of Dade, "teachers are tired, they've had a difficult year and they need time to recover."[20]

Annette Katz, Director of Media and Public Relations for the United Teachers of Dade, made it clear that teachers were not opposed to the new programs but simply disagreed with the timing of when they were being implemented. As she explained, "We want to slow the train down."[21] The extent to which teachers felt strongly about the need for the moratorium was underscored by the fact that in the union's history no single issue elicited a greater response from the teachers than their desire to have new programs temporarily put on hold in order to have time to recover from the impact of Hurricane Andrew.[22]

CONCLUSION

During the first months of the recovery from Hurricane Andrew, tremendous demands were placed on the school system and its employees to help the community return to normal. In general, the school system, under the leadership of Superintendent Visiedo, did a remarkable job. Despite this fact, very real problems emerged, which probably could only have been understood by actually living through the hurricane and the recovery process.

Unlike more limited disasters, Hurricane Andrew encompassed virtually all of the community. As a result, people who normally would assume the roles of caretakers and protectors were also often victims. This was true of many other public servants including fire fighters, police, and medical personnel, as well as the teachers and administrators who worked in the schools. The stress placed upon them was twofold in that they were required not only to deal with their own personal problems but also to cope with the recovery of their schools and the needs of the students whom they taught.

Anything that complicated the immediate task at hand—anything that demanded long term planning and implementation—was simply beyond the focus of many people who were meeting crises on a day-today basis in the schools. In the following chapters, we look again at the teachers and administrators in Ashe, Porter, and Pine Villa and reflect on the impact of the crisis on their ongoing work and involvement with students.

NOTES

1. Laurie Goldstein, "School Routine Soothes Andrew's Trauma," *Washington Post*, September 16, 1992, p. 4A.

2. Jon O'Neil, "Caribbean Elementary: Long Road to Repair," *Miami Herald*, Neighbors Section, January 3, 1992, p. 18.

3. Ibid.

4. Alessandra Soler, "Learning to Share a School," Neighbors Section, *Miami Herald*, May 13, 1993, pp. 18.

5. Ibid.

6. Jon O'Neill, "Perrine Elementary on Rebound," *Miami Herald*, October 11, 1992, p. 19B.

7. Niala Boodhoo and Alessandra Soler, "Redland Students Adjust and Wait," *Miami Herald*, Neighbors Section, April 4, 1993, p. 22; and Howard Kleinberg, "Support Restoration of Historic Redland School," *Miami Herald*, April 13, 1993, p. 7A..

8. Tananarive Due, "School Routine Helps Teachers Avoid Self-pity," *Miami Herald*, September 17, 1992, p. 1B.

9. Ibid, p. 2B.

10. Jon O'Neill, "For Music Teacher, Job Is Best Way to Hit High Notes," Neighbors Section, *Miami Herald*, January 31, 1993, p. 26.

11. Ibid.

12. Ibid.

13. Interview conducted by Sandra H. Fradd and Eugene F. Provenzo, Jr. with Faye McCloud, February 26, 1993, Miami, Florida. The following quotes in the text are from this interview and are cited in the text.

14. Minutes: "Dade County Public Schools Hurricane Andrew Recovery Plan," Special Conference Session, School Board of Dade County Florida, October 14, 1992, p. 9.

15. Ibid, p. 10.

16. Pat Tornillo, Executive Director, United Teachers of Dade, School Board of Dade County, October 14, 1992 School Board Meeting.

17. Interview with Sally Osborne, Nelson Diaz, Henry Fraind, and Jerry Salcines conducted by Sandra H. Fradd and Eugene F. Provenzo, Jr., Miami, Florida, December 16, 1992. The following quotes are from the Osborne, Diaz, Fraind, and Salcines interview (henceforth called ODFS Interview). They are cited in the text.

18. Tom Dubocq and Fran Brennan, "Stressed Out; Teachers Plead for Storm Relief," *Miami Herald*, September 25, 1992, p. 1B, 4B.

19. Ibid.

20. "Teachers Seek Delay in Programs," *Miami Herald*," March 5, 1993, p. 2B.

21. Ibid.

22. Ibid.

6

The Year's End at Bowman Foster Ashe and Gilbert L. Porter Elementary Schools

By early May, as the school year was drawing to a close, the rebuilding process throughout the southern half of the county seemed to go on and on. Most of the garbage and debris had been cleared away, but dwellings that were to have been ready by Christmas still lacked roofs, windows, fresh coats of paint, and landscaping. Repairs were proving to be more difficult than most people had anticipated. Even if the insurance claims were generous, finding competent contractors and workers was difficult. Traffic proved to be a constant problem, with people still commuting from the northern part of the county to their jobs in the south. Parents who had moved out of the hurricane zone into whatever housing they could find frequently found themselves transporting their children back to their old neighborhoods to be with their friends or to attend schools where they would feel more at ease. Even those people who had not suffered serious damage from the hurricane were still dealing with colleagues, friends, and family who were victims of the storm and were seriously stressed by the recovery process.

During the fall of 1992, many of the teachers were uncertain about their ability to cope with the pressures imposed on them by the hurricane. Most found themselves living from day-to-day—simply for the moment or the problem at hand. Surviving from one week to the next was an accomplishment. Talking too much about the past or the future seemed irrelevant, and perhaps even irreverent. "Lord, let me get through today. . . ." was the unspoken prayer of many. By the end of May, however, most of the teachers realized that they were in the home stretch. They were going to make it—perhaps not with the achievements and celebrations of previous years, but make it they would.

In terms of our three schools, Ashe, Porter, and Pine Villa, everyone was happy to see the school year coming to an end, to look forward to the change of pace promised by the summer, and to reflect on the events that had made the 1992-93 school year different from any other in recent history. People in the schools were at last willing to discuss their feelings and insights in May, when earlier in the year they had been reluctant to even consider them.

Throughout the school year we continued to visit the three target schools located at different points in the storm-damaged area. Because of the sensitive nature of the rebuilding process, interactions were limited to brief exchanges rather than lengthy interviews that might bring up difficult topics. In late May and early June we returned to the schools to conduct more in-depth interviews and to create descriptive pictures of the communities surrounding the schools. This chapter provides a summary of the rebuilding process that went on within Ashe and Porter and in the immediate communities surrounding them.

BOWMAN FOSTER ASHE

By June, the area around Bowman Foster Ashe had essentially been restored. At first glance, little evidence remained of the damage caused by the hurricane. Closer inspection, however, revealed many severely pruned or newly planted trees and houses that were still being reroofed and with general repairs and reconstruction still taking place. One significant indicator of the effects of the hurricane could be seen in the royal poinciana trees that abound in the area. In a typical June, these trees, with their thick trunks, large spreading branches, and fernlike leaves, are normally covered with flaming red and orange flowers. The flowering of the royal poincianas is so striking that many people take drives during late May and early June just to enjoy the splendor of the trees. In June of this year, few of the leaves had begun to unfold. Occasional orange or red blossoms could be seen peeking out on still stark branches. The recovery of the flora was an important part of the rebuilding process. The flowering of the royal poinciana seemed to symbolize the slow recovery. Like the people in the hurricane recovery area, the trees were struggling to return to a normal life, communicating a willingness, and yet a difficulty, in recreating life as it had been.

After the hurricane, Bowman Foster Ashe Elementary School was described as being "transformed from a quiet Kendall school into a hurricane haven."[1] In most of the two south county regions, Regions five and six, school enrollment decreased as a result of the storm. Ashe defied this pattern by receiving more than 250 additional students (a 29 percent increase) during the first week it opened in September, 1992. No other school in the county added so many students so quickly. According to Dr. William Koch, the school's lead teacher, "We had anticipated some growth. But the hurricane changed everything."[2] Koch said that the administration was prepared for some increases and had ordered sufficient supplies, desks, and texts for seventy-five additional students. The administrators and teachers at Ashe "made every student feel at home there, and that's a real gift. I credit the faculty and the leadership of the principal for that," said superintendent Visiedo.

Dr. Frazier Cheyney, the principal at Bowman Foster Ashe Elementary School, provided insight into the recovery process. Like the royal poinciana, Cheyney seemed to communicate a willingness to rebuild and recover, but his voice also revealed a tiredness and a sense of the frustration that he, the faculty, and staff had faced over the year:

> It's been a year of trying to keep the normal goals of the school system, the instructional programming. That part hasn't lessened one bit. There have been many new demands from the school system as far as improving instructional programming, adding additional programs into the schools. But, at the same time, much of our energy has been channeled in other directions. We have spent a great deal of time working with children who are very angry and very upset. A great deal of our time has been channeled into assisting them and their parents who often are equally as upset with the things that are going on. Much of our time has been spent in this area in addition to basic programming. It's been a very intensive year. We are really working around the clock to not only achieve the normal goals of the school, but also to take care of these other needs. It seems that the school institution, after we got back on the 14th of September, took the lead in the recovery process and assumed a lot of the responsibility for things that have happened since the hurricane. It's not the fault of the teachers, the principal, or the school system; it's just that we were there.[3]

For Cheyney, the situation faced by the schools was

> a bit like the motorists going from one place to another, when they come upon a bad accident with people lying all over the road. They can drive in between them to achieve their destination, or they can decide to stop to get out and help. Basically, that is what we are doing. The target or the goal that we have is instruction. But a lot of our energies have been dissipated performing these other tasks. The fact that our energies have been

expended in these other areas doesn't reduce the significance or the demand that we achieve our primary goal of instruction. (Cheyney Interview)

Both the Dade County Public Schools and the state of Florida had initiated a number of new programs to which the schools had to respond despite their experience with the hurricane. Many of the principals with whom we spoke mentioned the difficulties imposed by these initiatives when combined with the problems they had to handle as a result of the hurricane. As Cheyney explained:

> Blue Print 2000 is the main one. It's the one that's been most advertised because it calls for full-scale development of all the people affecting the schools—the teachers, the parents, the students, the business community, everybody. It's being written up in the newspapers as the program of greatest significance. But it's only one of many initiatives. Phoenix is another one. That's important because it does involve federal money and decisions are still being made as to how the money will be given out—who will receive it. Those two programs are the ones that have been given the greatest attention, but there are scores of other programs that come regularly, through e-mail and memorandums, requiring teachers to attend workshops, principals to develop programs, and teachers to develop new curriculums. The list goes on and on. (Cheyney Interview)

Seemingly the change process of school improvement grows exponentially—perhaps, as in the case of Project Phoenix, even as a result of the hurricane. Changes and innovations place new demands on teachers' and administrators' time. Some of these demands would have occurred whether or not there had been a hurricane. Because the school was still in recovery mode, however, the demands that were made were perhaps more strongly felt than if this had been a normal school year. Cheyney explained:

> These initiatives have the effect of creating add-on programs. Each program has value in itself. These are valuable programs, but it's just one other program that we are asked to do. There was no moratorium for developing new programs this year. When ideas come through and the school board thinks that they are good, then they are delivered to the schools. Some are not mandatory; some are required. Most of them are urged, strongly urged, so that there is some follow-up to see what has been done, even if it's not required. They expect us to pay some kind of attention to the program. A lot of them are mandatory by the school board or the state guidelines. (Cheyney Interview)

Sometimes it was hard to sort out the difficulties created by the storm from those that evolved as a result of instructional and administrative innovations. While there are many ways of dealing with problems in the schools, the school district's response to human needs was, in part, to create new programs. According to Cheyney:

> I think that with the addition of the problems of the hurricane, we are talking about the human area where people have been uprooted out of their homes and have experienced other kinds of difficulties. We have been pushed to really take care of these kinds of problems during school and through a lot of after-school programs, especially during the summer, in order to make up for the problems created by the hurricane. There are problems such as not enough movie theaters in the south end of the county, not enough parks to play in, so the schools have assumed that responsibility for the communities. (Cheyney Interview)

Integrating the changes while continuing with the recovery process was a balancing act that required a great deal of accommodation from both the teachers and the administrators. This was especially true in accommodating children with emotional difficulties. During an interview conducted in October, Cheyney stated that one of the greatest problems that he was encountering was with the high number of students who were attempting to run away from school. Many would look for ways to go home just to see if everything was alright, to be with their families, or just to escape the pressure of school. As the year progressed, emotional difficulties became visible in other ways:

> The intensity and problems have caused the children to come apart. You see this in different ways: the violence, the anger, the family problems. We are spending a lot of time on that because we have to. Just like the example of the car accident. We cannot leave the bodies lying about. We have to get out and help, do the best we can in that situation. (Cheyney Interview)

The school faced a serious challenge in working through the emotional problems of many children and their parents. These difficulties were brought about, in part, as a result of the storm. Other factors have also contributed to these difficulties. As Cheyney explained:

> There has been an increase in emotional problems far greater in proportion to the 30 percent increase of students in the school. This increase [in emotional problems] has to do with two things. We have a lot of new students in the school and they are learning how to get acclimated to our environ-

ment. They may have come from places where maybe fighting was the established rule for solving their problems. We've also come upon some parents, well . . . for example, we had one parent who actually organized a battle off campus between his son and another student to just duke it out and resolve some of their problems. We were able to stop that in time, but that's . . . [an example of] some of the attitudes that the teachers have been noticing in much greater proportion this year. Every school has cases of parents whose views run counter to what we try to teach at the school, such as that we don't get into fights because you can get hurt. That's what we've got. Many of these parents are new, new families coming in. The other factor has to do with the physical proximity of kids to each other. You put more kids in a room; you seem to have more difficulties. (Cheyney Interview)

During a period of time when the welfare of the students and their well-being was of critical concern, it seemed that central office administrators and people who had not been directly involved in the day-to-day workings of the school failed to see the difficulties that teachers and administrators faced. Concern about standards, test scores, and program policies appeared to take priority over effective instructional practices. According to Cheyney:

I just see so many people who are wondering about standards in the system. Are they slipping? Are you not as good as you used to be? Are you slipping? Are you doing all of these programs? There is a mandate from the school system. What are you doing about it? And here we are. We're just trying to stay afloat and these people have a piece of paper in their hands to justify every remark that they are making. It's like the policeman who is spit upon. You just sit there and take it. We can't react negatively to that. We are dealing with the public and with upper administrators. So you just sit there and smile and try to understand that they are doing what they feel that they have to, but it doesn't seem that they have an understanding of the kinds of things that we are dealing with well. We aren't doing all the things that people want. "You haven't done this. You haven't done that. What are you going to do about that?" they say. Perhaps in a normal year we could go into that, but this has not been a normal year. (Cheyney Interview)

Part of the balancing act of meeting students' and teachers' needs, while at the same time, complying with the system's requirements for information and record keeping as well as program implementation, was finding enough time during the school day to plan, to meet, and to organize. During the normal school year the teachers have ten professional days for completing school work, attending in-service meetings, and planning. This year the school calendar was changed, removing seven of the teachers' professional days to make up for the late start of the school year. The teachers had only one day at the end of the year to complete all their school record keeping. Although they also had two work days at the very beginning of the year, those days were used to clean up their classrooms and get things organized. "After that," Cheyney explained, "we just have not had time to get ourselves together, except on an individual basis." In spite of the lack of allocated time for meeting and planning, the schools have had to plan and meet the demands of new curricula from the district:

> We have had to have meetings during the school day. We've tried to keep the things that we do to a minimum at this school, but when things are required by the district, then we do meet. We get these things hashed out. It's my role to try to interpret these things and put them in a scheme that will lessen the impact on the teachers' time. I try, for example, to present things in forms that can be handed out instead of having meetings. It's been very difficult because it seems that there are always reasons to have meetings. And we have them. (Cheyney Interview)

Teachers were under a great deal of pressure in the year after Hurricane Andrew because of the loss of professional days, the need to resolve personal difficulties, such as home refinancing and rebuilding, and the need to aid children who were coping with emotional difficulties. Several solutions to time demands placed on the teachers and administrators evolved. According to Cheyney:

> A great deal of pressure has been put on the teachers to be absent, to take care of their own personal matters. Many times teachers take personal days and do their school work. Even some administrators have been doing that. The reason that they do that is that they can't do it while they are teaching children. Without any work days this year I've been opening the building on Saturdays and having teachers come in and spend three or four hours getting things done. With no students here, they can get a lot accomplished. I'm opening the school this Saturday because it is right before the end of the year. Teachers have been putting a lot of extra hours into their jobs. It has caused two teachers in this school to take a short-term leaves of absence. This may not be directly hurricane related but just a build up of a lot of personal losses and personal problems. They felt that they couldn't take care of it all and remain in school so they had to take

leave without pay to get things done. I suspect that other schools may have been affected more in that area. There have been a lot of absences, a lot of teacher absences this year. It's been running about five a day this year, where it has been normally one or two. (Cheyney Interview)

In considering what he might like to see done differently in the future, Cheyney reflected that "we have a large school system. We have to remember that half of the schools were not affected as we were by the storm." But for those schools that were affected, he suggested:

If there could be any moratorium on developing extra programs and push-ing right ahead, that would be helpful. Maybe trying to allow the park system to take on some of the responsibility for the kids after school, try[ing] to get them to move on that instead of putting it all on the schools [would help]. (Cheyney Interview)

The single most important aspect of recovery, Cheyney suggested, is the time the teachers need to take care of their own affairs and to attend to the noninstructional aspects of the educational process at school. Educators also need a time to rest and recuperate. Cheyney stated:

The teachers need to have the work days. They could have shortened Christmas, or spring recess, or added days on the end of the year. Maybe, in all fairness, no one realized that until after the fact. I realize that we are no longer a farming community. We don't need six weeks for kids to go out and help with the harvest. But there is substantial information about needing time to rest, letting the ground go fallow, letting people rest and recuperate. You just can't go continuously, continuously, and continu-ously. (Cheyney Interview)

According to Cheyney, approximately 10 percent of the faculty was typically absent on any given day. Faculty absences placed an addi-tional burden on the administration—it had to find substitutes to replace the teachers. Cheyney described this process, too:

We've had a lot of difficulty getting substitutes. We have a lot of substi-tutes in this area. Quite frankly, there are some that we tell to come every day so we know that we have a base of people who we can call on every day. Even then, we still have to call on people who we don't know. Most are successful. There are a few failures. We don't call them back again. We don't like to be in that position. The first year we had a few standby sub-stitutes who were qualified people who we knew could do the job. There were two people; part of the year we had three, so we had two or three standby substitutes. These were qualified people who came in, and we knew that the program would not suffer. The teachers knew the people and were able to plan with them in advance, maybe the previous day, and get things all settled, so instead of getting review work, the children could actually have instructional classes. This year I am afraid that we have had to rely more on back up and reviewing activities rather than substance. The teachers keep activities or substitute lesson plans, which they put to one side. When they return from their absence, they can come back and take up where they left off. (Cheyney Interview)

It may seem that because of the many absences the quality of instruction was not as high this year as during the past. Cheyney disagreed and strongly reaffirmed the dedication and capability of the teachers at Ashe:

If anything has slipped, it's the absences that could make things slip a little bit, not having the presence of a regular teacher. The teachers at this school are devoted enough that when they are here they put forth their full effort. If you think of people who have a lot of things on their minds, then perhaps, subconsciously, that is going to affect their teaching. That's very possible, but generally when the teachers are here, the teachers who I have seen are putting forth their full energy. They are not drawing into themselves because of the problems they are having. But I do know that they are having problems. They point it out in normal conversation. We don't find that out by seeing them slumped in their seats or just passing out papers to kids while they are doing insurance paperwork. You don't see that. They are functioning as they normally have, except for the two who were wise enough to recognize that they couldn't do everything. (Cheyney Interview)

There was a concern that the use of personal days and the growing number of absences could become a habit. This led Cheyney to underscore the need for the school and working conditions to return to normal:

I have to get this turned around so that when we begin school in the fall [1993], we go back to normal programming. The first year that we opened school, it was two weeks before we had the first teacher absent. Everybody was so anxious about opening the school that no one was absent. This year it has been tremendous. They have been absent since the 14th of September, the day the schools reopened. (Cheyney Interview)

The school system provided a great deal of support for the teachers. According to Cheyney, this support came in both formal and informal ways:

The support for teachers in the recovery process has come from two sources. From the district itself, we have the employees assistance program. They have been very helpful. They have sent out people to talk to our faculty about stress and other things related to the recovery. On an individual basis the district assists people by answering their questions, providing counseling, and so forth. At the school level, the things that we have been doing have been [of] more of an informal nature—helping each other, talking to each other. We have a social committee that's very active, providing the kinds of activities that ease people through. (Cheyney Interview)

Perhaps the administrative leadership, in the interest of making the schools effective places for children, did not realize the demands that were being placed on the educators at the south end of the school district. Perhaps, Cheyney suggested, the schools have created a facade, rather than a reality, of being able to keep up with demands:

I guess there is a fear that if we don't keep our instructional demands up, then we will slip down, and we'll never see them again, and we'll be a poor school system. What making these demands is doing is giving the appearance that we are really moving along in the area of instruction, when in fact, we just may be putting out the information that was necessary to give the appearance. We may be trying to placate some people so that we can get back to the real business, which is trying to deal with these kids, not just to teach them multiplication and fractions. But we are trying to deal with them as humans—trying to get them to stay in school, not get angry and be so violent and disrupt the program. You know that we are really working down at that level. When you bring in all these new programs and say "meet after school," "meet during school," and "we need to do all of these things," you wind up just burning out everybody. I would say that [too many meetings] and the fact that we had no breaks, even single day breaks, work days, would have been really useful. (Cheyney Interview)

In terms of plans for the future, Cheyney had several goals, all related to the overcrowding the school was currently experiencing. While a portion of this increase could be directly attributed to the hurricane, a large part of this growth would probably have taken place anyway as a result of the school's location. Cheyney's concern was that a plan be developed to address the school's boundaries and the number of anticipated students. The greatest concern that he expressed was for finding sufficient space for all the students:

My goal for next year is to make things as normal as possible. We did get a few FEMA relocatable buildings through the district. They are very beautiful. We can put four classes in there. We've got them all mapped out on how we are going to use them for next year. That may just get us through the first six months. I am sure we are going to have to ask for more portables for next year if we don't have a boundary change. Next year my goals will be to keep our classrooms as small as I can by making use of the spaces we have here so that we don't have all of the kids crowded into one room. That's my major goal. (Cheyney Interview)

Faye McCloud, the guidance counselor at Ashe who has shared her insights on surviving the storm and returning to work, compared the guidance services offered through her office during the first year that Ashe was opened, 1991-92, and those offered during the 1992-93 school year. This record also served to underscore the need for the faculty to work with the many troubled students attending the school. In May 1993 she prepared the following written summary:

During the 1991-92 school year, when Bowman Foster Ashe first opened its doors, the Guidance Program was an integral part of the new school from its inception. Referrals for guidance counseling services were made by teachers, parents, and students alike. From a student population of 835, 143 students were seen in weekly group counseling sessions. In addition to this some students were seen who were in crisis for a onetime counseling session with follow-up. Referrals most typically were for low self-esteem, poor peer relationships, low academic progress, and disruptive behavior. There was a preponderance of referrals for these concerns. Other referrals were for retention, withdrawn behavior, low motivation, poor attendance, poor school adjustment, poor social skills, children from dysfunctional families, and issues surrounding loss, grief, and depression. Primary children (grades K-3) were most frequently referred for guidance counseling services due to disruptive behavior, much of which could be attributable to young children's impassivity.

In contrast, the 1992-93 school year was a most unique and challenging year with a myriad of problems as a spin-off of Hurricane Andrew. When our school opened its doors three weeks late, it was with an additional 300 students in comparison to last year. Our population to date is 1,176 students [as of May 12, 1993] which is beyond our physical capacity. Bowman Foster Ashe sustained itself well against the wrath of Andrew, unlike other schools south and east of our location. Thus, we received students displaced by the hurricane. Our students experienced extended family existence with various and sundry living arrangements for the hurricane victims. The vast majority of our students were adversely affected by the hurricane. Homes and personal belongings were damaged and lost. As the sole guidance counselor at our school, I was faced with the monumental challenge of allaying anxiety and abating grief reactions (despite my own personal victimization [by] the ravages of the hurricane).

The referrals came quickly and without relent. Children benefitted from guidance counseling services via total classroom affective educational activities as well as short term group counseling. All K and 1 students received direct services through counselor visits to the classroom. Some of these students, pre-k and 2-5th grades were engaged in group counseling. Fifteen classes were seen weekly for one hour each, September through November, 1992. A total of 302 students were seen in short term small group counseling over the course of the 1992-93 school year. The most salient issue continues to be the ill effects of the hurricane. There have been a disproportionate number of children exhibiting aggressive behavior this year. The Hurricane Relief Team was dispatched to our school for a two week commitment which they recently completed. This cadre of four crisis counselors' final assessment was a recommendation for a second counselor to "contend with the deep hurt and pain found within these pretty walls." Without question, this school year has been unusually trying for students and staff as well. The upcoming hurricane season and its related anxiety only serves as an impetus to rubbing salt in a yet to be healed wound.[4]

While Ashe was one of the schools that did not sustain major physical damage, it is clear that it was profoundly affected by the hurricane. Losses on the part of administrators, teachers, and staff, as well as losses in the surrounding community, contributed to the difficulties posed by the rebuilding process. In addition, the relocation of many students from more severely damaged areas necessitated a redefinition of many aspects of the school as an innovative educational center. If for no other reason, the increased number of students changed the climate of the school.

GILBERT L. PORTER

Gilbert L. Porter Elementary School is located in an area known as the Hammocks on the southwest side of western Kendall Drive, just before the street dead-ends at Krome Avenue, at the eastern edge of the Everglades. While many of the stores and shops located along and just south of Kendall Drive were damaged by Hurricane Andrew, most were able to reopen within two weeks to a month after the storm. Even though this area still showed signs of the storm's impact almost ten months later, much of the damage had been repaired as commerce and a sense of community was restored.

In August 1992, when we first visited the school, there was destruction everywhere. All of the roofs in the development next to the school had, at the very least, many broken tiles. In some cases, roofs, walls, and windows were more seriously damaged. By June 1993, the homes in this particular development had been restored. All of the roofs had been replaced—rusty, Mediterranean red barrel roof tiles had been replaced by mottled shades of pink and gray tiles.

Around the corner from the school, in an area facing the Everglades, was another subdivision of more modest homes that appeared to be about three years old. While reconstruction was also under way in this area, at least a third of the houses showed no signs of renovation or occupation. Elsewhere, we saw many homes and apartment houses with roof damage, missing windows, and torn patios and pool screens. Some of the buildings still had the appearance of having been sandblasted or scoured by a more than a human force.

Principal Zerlin shared his insights on the 1992-93 school year. In considering the role of the school in the rebuilding process, he expressed a strong positive view:

> It's interesting how we are getting back together, slowly, but we are getting there. It's interesting to see the apartments next door. People are moving in again. I can see the enrollment moving up again. I see the homes across the street are being rebuilt again. What is really amazing, I keep thinking about it, the school had such little damage and all around us there was so much damage. That's what makes it great that the school was here for everybody. I think that the teachers did a wonderful job of making the families feel welcome. What I have been saying is that here, at this school, we have been the anchor of this community.[5]

The efforts of the school to rebuild and to assist the community did not come without considerable cost, as is evident when Zerlin described the commitment of school personnel:

> I never had so many personnel problems in one year. I am tired. The year has really had its ups and downs. It really has shown the tolerance level of staff. Many of the staff members have gone beyond the call of duty. Many of the staff lost their homes. A particular example, my secretary . . . the

hours she had put into this school. . . . The teachers and custodial staff, their tolerance level. I think, "Wow! What if Frederic Zerlin lost his house? Would he be able to cope like these people have coped?" The way that they handle children and community members is remarkable. (Zerlin Interview)

Progress was not smooth, as Zerlin was quick to point out. After the hurricane many students at Porter were also deeply troubled and in need of psychological counseling and support:

Thank God we had a crisis intervention counselor and she did an excellent job, along with our own counselor, working with the children's problems. We have had more children talking about suicide this year than I have ever heard of in my whole career. Maybe once or twice, but this time it was much more like fifteen to twenty—kids who were living in one room with their parents, kids living in a trailer, kids that were moved from one place to another, four and five times. [Many had] parents divorced, parents separated, since the hurricane. Those are the kinds of things—it was remarkable the stories that I heard. But we've coped; the children coped. We've turned a lot of these children around. We turned them around—their way of thinking about the hurricane. I noticed that the more that we talked about the hurricane, the better they felt and the more that they were able to understand it. Reflecting back, it has been a very trying year. (Zerlin Interview)

While teachers did not formally use personal days to catch up on school work as they did at Ashe, the teachers at Porter did demonstrate a need to have time to work on professional tasks beyond the regular school day. As Zerlin explained:

There were lots of personnel problems; people who wanted to take off at 12:00 and wanted coverage. One thing that I had to be was humane. But I also had to be the person in charge, and yet I had to let the people go, four, five, and six people in a day, every day. Absenteeism was definitely a problem. This year I had at least five to six people out a day, sometimes fifteen to sixteen out. (Zerlin Interview)

The elimination of the professional days, in Zerlin's opinion, was:

Awful! Awful! It was the worst thing that could have happened. The teachers in this school . . . needed time to get their things completed. I had a big problem this year with people working overtime [with] teachers [who] wanted to work on Saturdays [and] teachers who wanted to be here until 7:00 or 8:00 at night. Of course you are expected to teach all day, but you

have to get in the writing skills and all that [grading or scoring the writ-
ing].You can go into the parking lot now and see people here until 8:00 or
9:00 at night. I don't think that they should have taken the work days
away. The teachers needed those days. They were really tired. I think that
they should have let everything run as it was. (Zerlin Interview)

Because of the damage to the parks and play areas, Dade County
Public Schools devised a plan to assist students in the storm area to
find activities during the period between when the school was out for the
academic year and the beginning of summer school, several weeks later.
This year schools had the option of running an additional school period
referred to as "intersession." During intersession teachers would be
employed to provide students with recreational activities and fun, learning experiences. Zerlin indicated that there would not be an intersession
period at Porter, but that the school would respond to the needs of the
community in another way:

We are not doing intersession, but we are doing library. We will have the
school library open on Saturday and two nights a week. We used to have a
public library around the corner. I thought that it would be good for the
children to come in on Saturday or during the week during the intercession.
The public library is still closed. (Zerlin Interview)

Porter was paired with Pine Villa for more than a month, resulting in
double sessions as well as intense planning for both schools. In reflecting on that experience and the relationship that was fostered through it,
Zerlin affirmed it as a positive experience that continued to be shared
throughout the school year:

We offered to take Pine Villa, to help another school. I think that it was
wonderful. I'm glad that we did it. It was good for the kids to see a different type of area and [for] the Pine Villa kids to see this type of area. What's
good about it is that we have become involved with each other. During the
Country Fair we had both communities together. The parents got together.
I think that something good came out of it. I think that it made my kids say,
"Hey, I'm really glad to be here." The kids from Pine Villa, I think that
they were glad to get back and to make the best of their school, to get
back to a regular schedule. When the two communities got together, the
kids ran back and forth. I think that was the best for both groups. We plan
to continue the relationship next year. We'll have pen pals, writing back
and forth, field trips back and forth, fun days, kick ball games, competition
things. (Zerlin Interview)

In terms of support from the school system's central office, Zerlin stated: "I had no problems. As far as that goes, anything that I wanted or needed, I was able to get. I don't know if it was because we were paired with Pine Villa, but we had more people than we really needed to help us get started." In addition to the support from the school district, there were other sources of support for the schools impacted by the storm:

> We had so many donations from all over the country. Dade County Public Schools was helpful—giving out our name to different agencies. To tell you the truth, we got more than we really needed. I know that it was in part because of G.L. Porter and Pine Villa pairing. (Zerlin Interview)

Like Cheyney at Ashe, Zerlin also believed that it would have been helpful "not to worry about new programs this year. I didn't have the problems that schools further south of me had, but I had frustrations and I can understand their frustrations." Every time a new program came in, he said:

> I had to meet with the staff and tell them, "Hey, here's something new." Although I know that it was just the timing that was wrong . . . my school was one of the only schools that didn't want to stop it when UTD (the union) had the vote throughout the county for the moratorium. (Zerlin Interview)

In thinking about the recovery process in terms of employee needs, Zerlin reflected: "I think that the people who were left out of this whole process were the principals, the custodians, and the office staff. The principals and the custodians had to be here. The hurricane came through on August 24. On August 24 we had to be here to check out the school. We needed some time off."

In addition to conversations with the principal of Porter throughout the school year, Tarja Geis, the Saturn Coordinator, provided updates of school developments related to the recovery process. In late May 1993, we asked her to give us a summary statement about the year's events.[6] Her perceptions of the events of the school year follow:

> I think that in terms of the hurricane, initially we were all somewhat stressed and shocked, but because we knew that we had a job to do and we had to work with the children, the storm actually brought us closer together. It gave us greater goals than just the educational goals that we had established. The storm gave us the goal of bringing some normalcy into the

children's lives, soothing many of the rough edges, making things OK, and of giving the children a haven where they would feel safe. The same thing [happened] with the faculty. Many of us had our own problems. I'm still in a trailer. But that's one of those things we are just dealing with. It's been an experience that I think in a lot of ways has brought us all closer together and made us more understanding of one another. Maybe the storm has given us even more of a bond, a different type of a bond that we maybe didn't have before. We've always been a close faculty, but it gave us a chance to bond on a different level, a deeper level than we had previously experienced, a gut internal level. (Geis Interview)

In reflecting on the period of time during which Porter shared the school facility with Pine Villa, Geis talked about the importance of sharing:

It was great when we were able to share our school with another school because we had something to help someone else. Although many of our boys and girls were in really tough situations, the Pine Villa situation was so much worse in that area. It was good that we were able to bring them in and to share with them. One of the things that really impressed me was the many people who wanted to help. (Geis Interview)

With respect to the interactions with other schools in other parts of Florida and in other states, Geis observed:

We got care packages, warm fuzzies, notes and all sorts of wonderful things from all over. This also helped to create the bond that will go on. Some of our teachers and children are still communicating with other children in other states and schools. One of the closest ones was in the Carolinas where they were impacted by Hugo. Some of the schools there have stayed in communication with us. How deeply they felt. They were already a few years past what we were going through. They gave us support. They said, "You'll make it. We've survived. You will too." That sort of thing. They really understood and cared about us. Perhaps we did not need the physical and the monetary support as much as we needed the hug around our shoulders. (Geis Interview)

Thinking back to the time before the school first opened, she recalled:

At first the school was like a mountain of hope; it had survived. Right after the hurricane we all drove by just to see that it was still here. Once we knew that it was OK, it was almost as though the Band-Aids were put on other places, but what really counted was the school. This is part of our family, our extended family, and it had survived. I think the community felt the same way. The roofs came off and the windows blew through, but the school was there. For the children, that was really important. It's a big part of their lives. (Geis Interview)

During the school year, Porter served many different roles. We have tried to capture educators' insights as they worked through the year and became increasingly aware of the importance of the school in serving the community. Here Geis summarizes her perceptions of these important functions:

> The role of the school also served many other purposes as part of the extended family. We had nursing services here and FEMA had an office here. FEMA was especially here to help the teachers of both staffs. FEMA was also at Pine Villa to help the community there. They came here to help the teachers and the community members. They were housed in Mission Control [Central Office] and the Discovery Center [Library]. We usually have fund raisers. We decided not to have those sort of things this year. We had extra counseling, extra help of many kinds, extra ears and hands. We were as flexible as we could be because of the parents' schedules. If the parents were late, we tried to stay open as late as possible to help them. There was free food, breakfast, and lunch for everyone through January. (Geis Interview)

The school played an important role in supporting and unifying the community. According to Geis:

> [As] one of our first unifying events, we had a Thanksgiving dinner in November. We knew that a lot of the families still did not have a place to cook. There was a nominal charge for the dinner. Whole families came, grandmas and uncles; everyone was invited and everyone came. What a pleasure to do that and to be able to do that for the community, to give something back to the community. We had the dinner on a Saturday, and we held open house and also a field day at the same time. We normally have a country fair in January. This year we had it on May 1. We invited Pine Villa. Three bus loads of Pine Villa adults and children came. It was very nice and everyone enjoyed it. I don't think that our philosophy toward the community and the parents has changed, but it has brought us closer together. We have always been open, always thought of ourselves as one big family. We always felt fairly comfortable discussing needs and concerns. I think we may be a little more able to facilitate our ability to assist the community, but I don't think we have changed any, since we have always been open. (Geis Interview)

Summarizing the year's experience, Geis observed:

> This year, it's hard to put into words how we feel. Now that we are at the close of the school year, we feel good knowing that the survival rate is getting higher. All the time now you can hear, "Your house is done! You're almost ready to move in. Great!" There is a unity, a celebration, maybe more and more little celebrations as each person becomes reestablished. The children are settling back into normal. This began to happen after the [December] holidays. The children were happy to come back. The staff too. I don't think that we'll ever get back to where we were because so many things have happened. There will always be those memories. Personally, it's made me realize how fragile that life is and how unimportant some of these external things are. What is important is what's inside—friendship, family, the intangible things that can just disappear with mother nature. Fortunately, we are all OK. Most of our families are OK. The physical [world] will be rebuilt. The heart is the fragile part, but we have survived and become even stronger. (Geis Interview)

Besides administrators, in May 1993, we also talked to teachers at Porter. Joanne Edwards is a third grade teacher who shared some of her perceptions of the rebuilding process after the storm.[7] Her response was typical of many of the teachers whose first thoughts were of the children and their needs:

> After the hurricane, we tried here at G. L. Porter to have the school be the children's home, to be there for them. We tried to put things back to normal in their lives because they were going back to an environment that wasn't normal. We tried our best here [to] make the day here be just as normal as it would have been without the hurricane. So we went on with all of our special activities and programs. We did not cut back any of the activities that we had at the school. Along with that we provided extra counseling for kids that needed to express what they were going through in their private lives. (Edwards Interview)

Edwards's descriptions of instructional activities provide insights into ways that teachers work with students who have undergone a traumatic experience such as a natural disaster:

> We wanted them to feel free to talk about their experiences with their teachers and the counselor. We also had the students write about them. We spent a lot of time writing about and reading about the storm. And then, we wanted to let them know that we wanted them to get on with their lives. So we put a heavy emphasis at the beginning after the hurricane on writing

about the experience so that they didn't harbor any feelings inside or hold anything back. We asked them if they needed any help, to please let the teacher know. Then, we went on to try to make the school day be as much as normal as possible without putting a heavy emphasis on homework. We knew that the children went home to homes and trailers where they didn't have space to do their homework. At the same time we did not lower our standards because of the hurricane. And that's basically what we are still trying to do. (Edwards Interview)

In terms of her own situation, Edwards's response was typical of many other teachers who at the end of the school year had not completely put their own lives back together:

I'm still trying to survive. I'm going through the stress every day of trying to get the roofer to finish the job, but I didn't really try to bring any of my problems in to my job. I tried not to and I've always tried to hold back. I still came to school. I don't usually take many days off from school. And so I'm still coming to work even though I could use the time off for the rebuilding process. I'm trying to just get through this year and make it to the summer. I will concentrate on it then. I've pretty much put the things that I need to do personally in my life on the back burner and let my school come first because I know that the children do not like to have substitutes. I try to come as often as I can. I have formed a bond with these children. When I'm out, they want to know why. I try not to disappoint them. (Edwards Interview)

On sharing the school with the Pine Villa faculty and students, Edwards observed:

I saw a lot of tension in the Pine Villa staff. I don't know if it was because of the fact that they not only lost their homes, but they also lost their school, their home for the children. Although I worked with a wonderful lady in this room, I didn't see them coming together with us. We tried to make them as welcome as possible, but I just saw the tension. They did not want to be here. They didn't feel comfortable here. I think that a lot of that has to do with their background. They are coming from a school that does not have as many assets as we have here, and they are used to working under conditions before the hurricane where they don't have teacher workrooms and a paper cutter in every workroom. They don't have the phones and the bathrooms, all the things that we have here. I think that they saw the inequities that existed before the hurricane and to come here and to work under these circumstances [was difficult]. I just didn't feel as though they wanted to be here. Although we tried everything to try to make them welcome, we did not bond at all. (Edwards Interview)

In discussing the children's adjustment now, nearly eight months after the storm, Edwards observed:

> I think that children adjust to situations better than adults. They understand about the hurricane. But it's still there. Like the other day, it was a topic on Monday morning when they came in. They said, "Oh, did you hear about the storm on Friday night?" They talk about it, but they are more willing to adapt—OK, this has happened; let's go on with our lives. They actually bring in to me more of the frustration that their parents are showing them than their actual frustration. (Edwards Interview)

Melina Castillo was another Porter teacher with whom we spoke. Castillo is the English to speakers of other languages (ESOL) teacher for first through fifth grades, and the chairperson of special area services at Porter. Many of her students speak Spanish as their home language, but her classes also include students from many other language backgrounds. Because of the difficulty in communicating with the students in their home language and because many of them were not yet proficient enough to communicate in English, Ms. Castillo had to devise many different ways to move her students through the initial trauma experienced after the storm:

> In terms of the students, first of all, many of them had different experiences and we were able to have them talk about their experiences either through drawings or writing. Many children talked about being in the bathroom and waiting out the storm. When they came back on the edgy side, or nervous, you had to be more gentle. Many are still having difficulties. They have nightmares about the hurricane. The special counselor, Cathy Sands [the crisis intervention counselor], comes two to three times a week to see the children on an individual and group basis. There are a lot of things going on in terms of hurricane related problems, separations, or just not getting along. Many of the adult situations greatly affect the kids. Children may have been very normal before and now they may have regressed because of the situation. For some of the children who were learning English, the hurricane experience was just one thing to deal with. It put them farther away from, let's say, the goal of learning English. A case in point, I have a set of second grade twins from Paris, France. They moved to Miami three days before the storm. They did not speak a word of English and had to deal with the hurricane. As young as they were, there was a lot that they had to sort out. What is important—getting over the ordeal of Hurricane Andrew or learning English? They put learning on the back burner and dealt with the hurricane.[8]

In reflecting on the experience of sharing her school with Pine Villa, Castillo observed:

> Once we went back to a normal schedule, and this is not a reflection on the other school, the teachers were able to be back to normal, to meet with the families after school; the bonding happened. There was a short time that the other school was here, but it was a critical time when the children needed to have more of us. They needed to have us talking to them. Once the time came when we were back to normal, the children could come up to us on a frequent basis. I think we all got better. (Castillo Interview)

The rebuilding process has not been easy, but there are important signs of progress. Castillo stated:

> The teachers have had to go through a lot of problems. Many are still in trailers, not having their homes. Even though the teachers have been involved in their own problems, they have left them at the door and dealt with the children. I think that the teachers have handled it pretty well. There doesn't seem to be that horror in their face. We have gotten a lot of support from the parents, the administration, and each other. I think that we have come a long way. Usually our open house is held at night. But we didn't want to worry about the parents coming here at night, especially since it is still very dark. This area gets like a cave in the middle of the night; it is so dark without the street lights. We wanted to make it something that when they came in, they could see the teachers and stay all day and enjoy. There is a lot of camaraderie between the parents and the teachers, to say we're all in this together. We have to get to work together. We did it on Saturday. We stayed here all day long. We had a time of camaraderie; we work together for the sake of the kids. (Castillo Interview)

Castillo's comments may make the rebuilding process seem easier than it actually was. The first week after the hurricane her room looked much better than it did on the day in May when she was interviewed. On that day, and for many weeks prior to it, heaps of books and papers were piled on every available table as the floors and closets were being repaired and recarpeted. As a result, the children were crowded together at tables placed so closely together that they could hardly get to their seats.

Although Porter sustained relatively light damage compared to other schools, like Castillo, the rest of the faculty had to work around the restoration process for the entire academic year. Carpets, tiles, and baseboards were removed from every room. Boxes of materials were everywhere. Equipment and facilities were not accessible because of the reconstruction process. Our research was interrupted several times because the rooms were being worked on or because materials from another room were being stored there. Sometimes the noise from the jackhammers removing floor tiles made communication difficult. The teachers were constantly aware of the restoration process as it impacted on their schedules and plans. They voiced concern about the completion of the process, but they also indicated that they understood and accepted the noise and the inconvenience. There was a minimal amount of complaining. Most of the discussion was reflected by a comment Castillo said with determination and a smile: "We manage."

For Mayra Huffman, the fourth and fifth grade science teacher, whom we met on the first day of school, the 1992-93 school year was seen as being particularly difficult for the children:

> I still have one child coming from the Homestead area over here. He's still living at Grandma's house or at mother's house. He's in between homes. I'm sure that it's because of the hurricane. I've asked them; most of them have their houses ready (meaning that they can now live in them). They (the students) hardly ever talk about the hurricane. I'm the one that doesn't have her house ready yet. I think that for most of the students it's not an issue for them any more although somebody brought up the fact the other day that June's coming around and they had heard it mentioned about storms and hurricanes on the TV. [9]

Teachers like Huffman were very aware that the trauma of the hurricane was an ongoing process for many children. This was particularly true when a major storm struck in March 1993. Referred to as the "Storm of the Century" because of the strong winds and damage it caused, the storm brought back memories of the hurricane for many people. Huffman remembers how she and the students reacted:

> When we came back to school, we talked about fears. . . . The children were scared all over again. I was also petrified. I have that phobia. . . . I never used to be afraid of storms. Now I'm very easily upset by any little storm. All this mess that is happening in the Midwest. I looked at that and I felt devastated. I just can't deal with it. I can't stand looking at it on TV. It's terrible! When the "Storm of the Century" was here, we were in our house in Key Largo. That thing was shaking like you can't believe. I was so scared. I could hear the noise. I could hear it coming. I could just smell it. I was telling my husband, "I am so scared!" (Huffman Interview)

During all of this, Huffman was concerned that school played a positive role in the students' lives, helping them in getting their lives back to normal. As she explained:

> I think that we (the school) have been good. Most of the teachers here have lost our homes. We've been struggling. But we have put that behind us. I have always told my children, "I'm in the same boat too. I'm sleeping on the floor, but I'm here at school every day." We have always had that attitude, the eagerness. But let me tell you it's hard. The school, the principal, everybody is very happy when we come here. We're supposed to be separated from all of that stuff because you don't see destruction. You have all the materials, and the beautiful new landscaping, the butterfly garden. (Huffman Interview)

At the same time, the school helped the teachers return to a more normal life and schedule. Huffman explained:

> To me, it's an escape to come to work. I leave the mess behind. When there's a box in the way, I kick it. I've learned to live with that. Nothing bothers me that much any more. I used to be super meticulous. Everything had to be in order. Now I know, it's still going to get done, but I know that it will come. (Huffman Interview)

Talking about the kinds of things that she did at first to help the children, Huffman found that the transition from dealing with the storm to general academic instruction was not as difficult as she had anticipated:

> I thought that it would be a long, ongoing process. It really wasn't. By the end of the first week, when I gave them another assignment related to the storm, I could hear "Oh! no! not that again!" I realized that maybe I was bringing back too many memories. Then I just cut it. Now, any time that there is a tornado warning or anything like we have had, or when there is bad weather, even a cloud, we all talk about it. Any time there is a little bit of wind, any little disturbance that is not normal, they talk about it. Or they will ask me, "How's your house coming along?" Or I will say, "Gee, I got a new bed today. I'm not sleeping on the floor any more." I may initiate something or nature may initiate something, and we talk about it. (Huffman Interview)

For Huffman, and many other teachers, there simply came a point where the storm needed to be put aside. Despite the fact that she had her children talk through their feelings about the storm, by the end of the year Huffman did not agree with the notion that it was beneficial for children and adults to talk about a tragedy in order to get over it: "I'm beginning to think that it isn't. I think that having had the same experience provides a bond, . . . we have something very important in common, but we don't have to talk about it too much," she said. "Perhaps talking about it may elevate rather than alleviate any pain. I think that we don't alleviate anything; we just pound the wound because they will think about it." Huffman continued:

> I've noticed that when the children think about the storm, they get more upset. They start to remember the things they lost. They may say something like, "Gee. Yea. I lost my Nintendo with that stupid storm." Then they get upset. You can bring back old wounds. So it's like me. I don't even want to look at the pictures that I took. I think just once, getting it out [is enough]. With these kids, by the end of the week when I gave them another assignment, they were like hysterical. (Huffman Interview)

Mayra Huffman is a teacher who exudes enthusiasm. Her ready smile greets children and adults alike. Yet, in spite of her positive attitude, there was an undercurrent of pessimism in her conversation with us. In this context, she recalled saying to her brother after the storm: "Why am I worried about cleaning all of this mess? The next one is going to come and take it away all over again." (Huffman Interview)

Huffman described herself as changing her attitude towards things as a result of the storm. Recalling her own personal experiences during the storm, she concluded:

> Nothing means anything to me any more. We stayed home and we saved a lot of valuables, but that was so selfish. . . . We were endangering our lives. We didn't think about that because my husband said, "I've been through hurricanes before." Everybody said the same thing. . . . I wanted to leave. I wanted to go to the hurricane shelter. He said, "No." When we were in the little bathroom and I was hyperventilating, we had the cushions over our heads and I was crying and screaming. He was doing everything he could to keep me comfortable and [to] make sure that nothing else blew away. He said, "You know, we should have gone. I had no idea that this was going to be like this." Thank God that our roof didn't blow away, but it lifted. And then the rain came in and then all three of my sliding glass doors went. . . . I could care less about anything. Since that experience, I have really lost interest in a lot of things that used to be important to me. (Huffman Interview)

As we were conducting our interviews at the end of the school year at Porter, we also had the opportunity to talk with Sharon Hine, an

ESOL teacher who lives and works in the Hammocks area. She is employed at Hammocks Middle School about five blocks away from Porter. She contributed insights regarding the rebuilding process throughout the year. One of the recurrent themes she expressed in other interviews during the year centered around her depression at having to deal with all of the ugliness in the area, in addition to all of the basic difficulties of trying to rebuild her home and her school, and just the difficulties she faced dealing with each day. Her observations provide a summary of what many teachers expressed over whether things would ever get back to normal:

> Here we are at the end of the semester and I find myself burned out. Now comes the really intense part of summing everything up. I still need to give my students their final exams and score them. . . . I am taking two courses at the University of Miami and I have finals there. Next week I start my new university courses. On top of everything I'm waiting for the contractor to do my house. He was supposed to start during Easter vacation but keeps pushing it back. Last week I got so depressed about my house and my school both being in the same condition. Both are functional. Everyone is still in the building, but things are filthy. Nothing works right anymore. It's depressing. So I called the contractor. But after I talked to him, I felt so bad for the guy. I felt worse for him than for me. He was so depressed. I thought that we should put together a support group for contractors. I like the guy. We've developed a rapport. But everything is just so depressed.[10]

A somewhat different perspective was provided by the school's counselor, Curtis Jenkins. When we talked with him, one of the first questions he addressed was the difference between the numbers and types of referrals received at Ashe and Porter before and after the hurricane. As he explained:

> It's hard for us to compare the types and frequency of referrals we have had this year and last because last year we had just begun to set up our system and the process hadn't really been formalized. There is a big difference in the referrals between this year and last year because of the unique way of doing things, dealing with teachers, and the curriculum that we are establishing. It's a dynamic process and we are modifying the process as we go along. Last year we were still learning to speak to each other and work with one another. . . . I found myself circulating and taking care of things more informally at first, much more than now because of the sheer numbers. When we first started, we had less than 650 and by the end of the

year we were capped at 650. That's a far cry from the over 1,000 we have now. The second thing is that we are feeling several impacts because of the storm: some are initial; some are delayed responses; some are compounded kinds of reactions, because not only of the storm, but also the subsequent things that people had to deal with—trash, contractors, families. One of the things that I think that would be important to note and to follow up on is the fact that the stress and related kinds of impact exacerbated . . . dynamics that were going on in families throughout the community.[11]

These differences between the circumstances of the two academic years for both Ashe and Porter do not diminish the concerns that the students and the faculty experienced, but they do make quantification of specific needs more difficult than if the schools were already well-established. Jenkins underscored one of the most important aspects of the rebuilding process, that is that the difficulties encountered after the storm did not always come about just as a result of the storm. Many of the difficulties were already there—faults in the structure, so to speak. The storm may have made the faults worse but did not necessarily cause them. Jenkins explained:

If there were difficulties in terms of dynamics, under regular circumstances people would go along their way and not necessarily lead to a separation. I believe that those dynamics are strained to such an extent that we are seeing more separations. That's just an example. In addition, there is the personality of the individual, that a person could handle stress under normal circumstances but . . . not just stressed to the limits. We see a lot more hostility with individuals, a lot more acting out in kids, that's almost directly and observably related to the stress that has come out of the storm. I think at the same time, it would be difficult to quantify. (Jenkins Interview)

Just as there were differences in people, there were also differences in communities, and in communities' responses to the storm. According to Jenkins:

It's important to focus on initial impact and the timetable and process for dealing with impact. . . . We got a good deal of damage, but I think that initially the people in this community were relieved that they weren't as badly damaged as people further south. But as time went on they were the ones that felt left out of some of the help that was being given. That initial relief of feeling safe went away because although they could stay in their houses, they had to sustain the drips, living on a concrete floor without some of the furniture, without some of the kids' toys and other creature comforts. While the initial impact further south was more devastating at first, the people down there could get some sense of relief and sense of progress, while [for] the people in our community . . . there was a long time when they had no sense of progress. And even now, they are still moving slowly along in the rebuilding process, almost as if it had no end. (Jenkins Interview)

Like Huffman, Jenkins provided personal insight into the rebuilding process by discussing his own experience:

My house was located on the north wall as the storm passed over. We still have stud walls. . . . We do have a roof. The shingles and doors are on now and we do have windows now. Since the storm, we have been living at my mother and father-in-law's house near Tropical Park. There are factors in the reconstruction process that are balancing acts. I feel that it is very fortunate to have the support of family; just the fact that someone else is making dinner, for instance, is very helpful. The in-laws tend to be very understanding about it and they feel that their contribution to us is a contribution to the whole community process. But living that close together with people who, even in a loving relationship, have different ways of living, is extremely difficult. It gets more difficult as time goes on. Each person needs to have some relief. We take different trips, and we try to do things that will help all of us maintain a sense of family. It's difficult to say just when all of this is going to end. The contractors keep extending the time. We are getting relatively short with them in terms of our tolerance. We have met with them recently. We should see some progress soon. One of the last inspections should happen today, in fact. The previous one was on the first of April. They needed to get some information so that the inspection could be held again. They kind of lagged on that so that held up the process. That kind of dynamic is difficult for us because, . . . both my wife and I, we like to deal with people in their professional capacities, without threats. It gets down to that sometimes. I would rather that people do it just because they have committed to do it. But it doesn't always work that way, particularly now when people are overcommitted and they say things to please people rather than with any sense of timetable. They told us initially that we would be in by Christmas. Then we asked them for a more realistic timetable and they told us the end of April. Now they have told us after this most recent round by the end of May. We're expecting to be in probably by the end of June. (Jenkins Interview)

Life following the hurricane has not been a simple, straightforward process of recovery. As Jenkins summarized his own experience, he provided insight into what many others have also said:

I found that the process was almost like a roller coaster, both individually and in terms of the community. Thinking about the contractor and all the problems of our own rebuilding, some days it was all that I could do to come to work. I think that was born out by the people that I talked to as well. (Jenkins Interview)

Jenkins believed that there were several the major disruptions during the school year. From a community point of view, one of the greatest was the difficulty of Porter being on double session:

> I think that there was a worry in the community that their kids would be impacted by Pine Villa in terms of sheer numbers—having their kids behind perhaps because there were so many kids in one space...but that was exaggerated. I think that Pine Villa provided for us a needed way to contribute. I think that even parents realized it after awhile, that it was not only beneficial for the kids and the staff from that community, but also for our kids and staff. I think that having Pine Villa here was an inconvenience only in terms of what we were used to. I don't think that it was an inconvenience in any way insurmountable by any means. . . . I think that it was difficult for the Pine Villa people, from what I was able to observe while they were here, because they had to deal with some of their difficulties, both in terms of children and of staff from a distance. Preexisting conditions, both personally and physically for them, in terms of their buildings and homes, was exacerbated because of the storm as well as the fact that they were some distance from their school site. They didn't have a sense of accomplishment for whatever was happening with their building, even as small as it was, because they were so far away. I think that some of the staff dynamics were stressed and strained because of the additional stress of the storm, the move, and being paired with a school. Using other people's space makes you almost certainly like a visitor, almost like an intruder. (Jenkins Interview)

For Jenkins, the recovery process was highly nebulous. No one really knew what to expect because no one had been through the process before. It was clear that everybody's stress level was raised substantially. The stress was so high that people saw things as insurmountable or as crisis situations that under regular circumstances would have been handled easily. Jenkins saw himself, for example, having parent conferences that used to take fifteen minutes, now take an hour. As a counselor, he found that what parents really wanted was reassurance that they and their children were alright, even when they did not feel OK.

As the school year evolved, there were discrete, predictable stages of recovery that the community, as well as the school, experienced. The first was the opening of the school year. The second occurred during the

Thanksgiving and December holidays. Jenkins described how when the December holidays approached, people initially had greater difficulty coping:

> There was an initial period when people felt relieved. Then, as we approached the holiday season, people began having the feeling that they weren't making progress. The holiday season, whatever holiday the people were observing, was a demarcation that their life was not normal. Things in their lives were not normal this year. They realized that they weren't going to have a holiday like they had before and that worried them. It bothered them that they couldn't provide for their kids or for themselves [as] before. Their traditions were not going to be the same this year. For different people there were different focuses, although they were much the same in the core. That really began to hit us. The peak was just before the holidays. After the holidays, people were forced to deal with the fact that they were going to have to deal with the issues. Perhaps they realized that they had more strength than they initially realized. We saw a difference when they came back after the holiday season. They were forced to deal with it and they found that it was OK because they had no control over the storm or the impact the storm had given them to deal with. They made the best of what they could. In many cases, families got together, several families together, for celebrations. Maybe they didn't get to Aunt Mildred this Christmas but they had Christmas, with the Jones next door. They found that was OK with them, and with the kids, and that once the kids felt comfortable, this sense of comfort started to spread itself. In the months after the holidays there was a perceptible change. After the holidays the focus changed from the personal to the academic concerns. (Jenkins Interview)

As the teachers, staff, and students at Porter went through the recovery process, so did the community itself. As Jenkins explained:

> We're in a community where people feel very strongly that they ought to be able to handle it themselves. These people, our community, is a community, for the most part, professional people in their career who are decision makers, doers. Even in the organizations that they belong to, they want to make an impact on the community. Kendall Federation is a very strong community oriented group, for instance, within the community at large, not even talking about the group like the Kendall Home Owners. In the PTA, these are people who want to contribute; they want to be able to do—doers. They were shaken by the hurricane. Through the whole process, their world, really their reality, including their perceptions, their reality was so shaken that they weren't sure about their capabilities, about their impact, or how much they could contribute. They

still felt the need, but they weren't sure how much they were accomplishing. If they could get a sense that what they were able to accomplish and the seeds that they were planting all through the process were the ones that needed to be planted, when they could see that they were beginning to be very productive, that's when we began to see fewer crisis kinds of conferences and fewer really critical referrals and acting out. . . . Toward the end of February and the beginning of March, it was getting better. (Jenkins Interview)

After the 1926 hurricane there was a strong sense of cooperation that helped to pull the Miami community together. As Miami grew and expanded and it changed from a small town to an urban metropolis, this sense of community changed and all but disappeared. After Hurricane Andrew, the schools provided an ideal place for reestablishing something of this sense of community. At the very least, schools became a rallying point for families and other concerned citizens.

At Porter, the school's role in reestablishing community was clear with the school's Thanksgiving dinner and Country Fair as centerpieces for community involvement and participation. Porter also had other activities, such as a parent day and a track meet. These events and the school's academic programs provided a haven—a place that was normal—in a storm struck culture. As Jenkins explained:

At the very initial impact of the storm, the school was a place, particularly our school by not being terribly damaged, where things could be sort of normal. There was a place that you could go and you knew that you were going to have math in the morning and reading in the afternoon. You knew that the teacher was going to be there and that somebody who cared about you would be there to greet you. All of those things added to the sense of security, initially, and even as the process for the community became more difficult, when the rebuilding began to wear on the community and the holidays were approaching, the information that we could give about the students, that they were OK, that these were things that could be expected— I think that those were helpful. The back-to-school night and the whole community could come to the spaghetti dinner, track and field day, parent days, and the country fair—[they] all involved the community. (Jenkins Interview)

For Jenkins, the school became a rallying point where people in the community could come together for support and interpersonal exchanges. The schools became an important place for talking and sharing. At the end of the school year, as Jenkins saw the progress that the school and the community were making, he found himself more open and available to reflect on the rebuilding process from the perspective of future planning.

> We're at a vantage point now where we can see the progress that's been made, but I'm not sure that we can see the whole process. A lot of things are still changing in terms of the dynamics, but if we had talked earlier, a good deal of what I understand now I could not have talked about earlier. We are at a strategic planning point now where we can direct things now rather than respond to them. The community is now at a point where they are ready to move and they need some direction. This is a critical point. The school can provide a leadership role, but only as much as the community is ready to work with the school and the two are committed to working together. We are at a point where we need to plan, not forget about the storm, but plan for the positive outcomes that we want to achieve. (Jenkins Interview)

CONCLUSION

The interviews conducted at Ashe and Porter at the conclusion of the school year revealed the important roles that the teachers, administrators, and support staff played in the rebuilding process. These individuals were highly committed to the students, their families, and the school/community relation ship. However, most of the educators had also experienced the storm and rebuilding process firsthand. Their own problems and personal concerns were no different from those of the children and families they served. There were no saints, but instead real people facing the challenges of many difficult circumstances. They, like many other service providers in the community, suffered through the storm, and yet, after the storm, were expected to reestablish normalcy. Having this type of demand placed upon them may have made the recovery process for them much more difficult than it would have been in earlier times, such as the 1926 hurricane. The question must be asked: While the school and its teachers are watching and supporting the children after a crisis like Andrew, who is watching over and supporting the teachers, counselors, and administrators who are making the school's recovery possible?

When schools like Ashe and Porter must assume the role of rebuilding community, they must of necessity relinquish—or at least de-emphasize—their role as educational innovators and leaders. The hurricane had significant consequences on the infrastructure of these schools.

While school and community links may have been strengthened, the impact of the rebuilding process may have pushed teachers and administrators away from their role as innovators and agents of change.

NOTES

1. Jon O'Neill, "Silver Lining: Hurricane Experience Forges Bond at School," *Miami Herald*, Neighbors Section, February 11, 1993, pp. 1, 18, 20.

2. Ibid, p. 18.

3. Interview with Frazier Cheyney conducted by Eugene F. Provenzo, Jr., May 1993, Miami, Florida. The following quotes in the text are from this interview. They are cited there.

4. Personal written communication, Faye McCloud, May 1993.

5. Interview with Frederic Zerlin conducted by Eugene F. Provenzo, Jr., May 1993, Miami, Florida. The following quotes in the text are from this interview. They are cited there.

6. Interview with Tarja Geis conducted by Eugene F. Provenzo, Jr., May 1993, Miami, Florida. The following quotes in the text are from this interview. They are cited there.

7. Interview with Joan Edwards conducted by Sandra H. Fradd May 1993, Miami, Florida. The following quotes in the text are from this interview. They are cited there.

8. Interview with Melina Castillo conducted by Sandra H. Fradd,May 1993, Miami, Florida. The following quotes in the text are from this interview. They are cited there.

9. Interview with Mayra Huffman conducted by Sandra H. Fradd, May 1993, Miami, Florida. The following quotes in the text are from this interview. They are cited there.

10. Interview with Sharon Hine conducted by Sandra H. Fradd, May 1993, Miami, Florida.

11. Interview with Curtis Jenkins conducted by Sandara H. Fradd, May 1993, Miami, Florida. The following quotes in the text are from this interview. They are cited there.

7

Pine Villa Elementary School

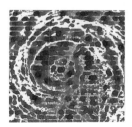

Located in the small and isolated municipality of Goulds, Pine Villa Elementary School presents a different picture from Ashe or Porter. Goulds—an historically African-American community—was established as the need for agricultural labor in South Florida grew during the early decades of the century. Pine Villa was built in 1959 during the initial period of racial integration. It has grown over the years to become a school with many portables, as well as its original two-story concrete structure. The school property is bordered on the north by housing developments, on the west by Mays Middle School and on the east and south by single family dwellings. U.S. Highway 1 is one block to the west. Cutler Ridge Shopping Mall and the Florida Turnpike are within walking distance of the school. Some of the teachers at Pine Villa have been at the school long enough to have taught three generations of children growing up in Goulds. Many of the first students they taught are now the parents and grandparents of their current students. Ties to the community are strong.

Today, the definition of the town of Goulds is more legal than visible. While for many years Goulds was a small town, apart from the big city, in recent years it has become part of the outer fringe of urban sprawl for the greater Miami area. In the process of evolution from rural to urban, Goulds has taken on some of the characteristics of an inner city ghetto. Many of its residents, who have lived all of their lives in the community, have witnessed the changes in the area and are acutely aware of the external forces that frequently seem to control their lives and their community. The most recent of these forces was Hurricane Andrew.

In this chapter we discuss the rebuilding of Pine Villa and the role of the school in reestablishing the local community. The story is both similar to and different from the experiences at Ashe and Porter. Both the similarities and differences are important because they reflect basic issues in the local culture, as well as in society at large. These comparisons are important because they underscore that the reality of the hurricane experience was not the same throughout the southern part of the county but experienced differently depending on geographical and socioeconomic setting.

Pine Villa was paired with Porter for more than a month, from September 14 through October 16. While this pairing was not as long as that experienced by some of the other schools after the hurricane, it imposed a type of regimen on the two schools that both were happy to change once their normal school day schedules were resumed. During the month in which both Pine Villa and Porter were housed in the Porter school plant, school reconstruction work was being carried out all over Regions five and six. Because of the large number of buildings that needed to be quickly repaired, both the laborers and the materials to make repairs were scarce. Pine Villa was therefore particularly fortunate to have received special help from the Canadian Air Force and Navy, which sent a contingent of engineers and craftsmen to assist in the rebuilding process. These highly trained and skilled military men spent nearly a month working at Pine Villa Elementary School, as well as adjoining Mays Middle School, repairing roofs, rebuilding stairs, replacing windows, and even fixing many of the computers and other technological equipment that had been damaged in the storm.

In addition to the help provided by the Canadian military, semi truckloads of food and other supplies were donated to people in the Goulds area by high schools in the Toronto area. On September 28, a special ceremony was held at Mays Middle School to express the school district's gratitude for the contributions the Canadians had made. The ceremony was concluded with Canadian Sea Bees serving hot dogs prepared on a gas grill they had brought with them for the occasion. Since only limited electrical services were available at the time and no restaurants were open for business in the area, the grilled hot dogs and punch that were served were welcomed as an enjoyable change by all who attended the ceremony.

After the ceremony, we toured the still unopened Pine Villa School. It was our first visit to the school since the hurricane had struck. There, we were able to see firsthand, even after more than a month of rebuilding efforts, the difficulties that lay ahead for the Pine Villa teachers and staff. A light rain began to fall during an already grey day as we walked through the old two-story building and its adjacent grounds.

There was destruction and confusion still evident throughout the complex. "How could the teachers and the students return to this?" was our question to Melvin Denis, the school's principal. "Oh, we'll find a way to make it work," was his reply.

Whether or not the school was ready, the fact was that the teachers, children, and parents at Pine Villa wanted desperately to return to their school. For many, returning represented getting back to normal. Sharing the rooms and resources of a new school more than ten miles away from their community was a difficult experience for Pine Villa—even though they appreciated the hospitality and friendship they were extended by the Porter community.

As the time for Pine Villa to reopen approached, one of the Pine Villa teachers expressed the appreciation that many of the faculty felt for the help and support they had received from Porter. The teacher's thoughts were published in a letter in the editorial section of the *Miami Herald*:

> On behalf of the Pine Villa Elementary School faculty, staff, and student body, I thank the entire Gilbert Porter Elementary family for being so kind and understanding. The assistance that we have received from these outstanding individuals has made a difficult transition into an energetic atmosphere for both schools. We are not sure how long it will take for Pine Villa to return to Goulds. But until that time, we have been made comfortable and given the boost needed to be able to maintain a motivational education environment. The Pine Villa students are very enthusiastic about their existing classrooms, and the faculty and staff feel quite fortunate to have found such a caring elementary school at Gilbert Porter.[1]

When school started in September, the date for moving back to Pine Villa had not been established, although it was anticipated that it would occur some time in October. As October came, there was speculation that the day would arrive soon, but it was not announced until just a few days before the move actually occurred. The dates and the reasons for the move were the sources of much discussion. It was rumored, for example, that the Pine Villa teachers had complained so much about being unhappy, that the administration had decided to speed up the move to stop the complaints. We never spoke with anyone at Pine Villa who indicated that he or she was unhappy at Porter, but several people told us about others who were unhappy. According to the informants, the main source of this rumored unhappiness was the need to have one's own things in one's own space.

TALKING TO THE
PINE VILLA TEACHERS IN OCTOBER

On Friday, October 16, Pine Villa began the moving process. Textbooks and supplies were boxed up once again and loaded on trucks to be unloaded and unpacked at Pine Villa. As the moving process was underway, we returned to Porter to interview some of the Pine Villa teachers and administrators about their perceptions of the move.

While the move was carefully organized and executed, it was clear that for the teachers at Pine Villa returning to the Goulds community was at least as stressful for them as their arrival at Porter. Our interviews with the teachers occurred in a small storage room piled high with boxes. A number of teachers participated in the interview—some for the entire time we were at the school, others for briefer periods of time.

The interviews were interrupted by a number of people entering and leaving, requesting information, and reporting events. As we spoke, the loudspeaker issued forth periodic announcements and gave directions to guide the teachers and movers.

For the teachers whom we interviewed, the hurricane was still a very fresh experience. For us, this was the first real opportunity that we had had to speak with the Pine Villa teachers at length since the hurricane. As with all of the interviews with the Pine Villa teachers, we have at their request removed identifying information about the participants. Because there were a number of participants, the dialogue is shown as a series of voices. One teacher explained how she felt very positive about her experience at Porter:

> We've become very attached to being here, and comfortable during this period of time. And now it's like going back to something. . . . I'm not really sure what's there. I saw the school after the hurricane. It's very damaged.[2]

Another teacher explained:

> I saw Pine Villa the day after the storm. I saw my room. There wasn't a wall. We have gotten really comfortable here. I'm really almost afraid of

what Monday at Pine Villa will bring. I know that I am going to have to do some accepting. I've had to make a decision, "Do I want a job? or Do I want to do the job?" I want a job and I want to do the job. I'll have to be alright with me so that I can do the job, so that the children will be alright. We'll have to make do. It has truly been an experience. We have had to deal with all kinds of personalities, and we have our own personalities. And we have all had to learn to come together.

When asked to elaborate about her experience at Pine Villa in the first days after the storm, another teacher explained:

> It was scary—scary with the National Guard, and the Red Cross, and helicopters flying above it and military men taking charge. I was out in a portable that collapsed and the military took me out to my room to load my car. It was like out of a movie.

New voice:

> I was there the Tuesday, the day after the storm. I had to do a body check. I had to go to my friend's home and my parents' home. I had to see that everything was alright. Then I asked my husband to take me to my school so I could see it, my other home. When I saw it, I started crying. I didn't know what to do or what to say or what to feel. I started worrying about the children. Where were the children? Where would they go? Everything was crushed and broken. It was sad because the children were outside crying; their mothers were outside walking around not knowing what to do. They felt what I felt. It wasn't a color thing or a rich thing. It hit everyone: the same emotions, the same loneliness, the same sadness. But also everybody was helping everybody too.

New voice:

> In my case, I was out of town, and I had prepared myself for the condition of my house. I knew that the house was still standing. It wasn't really that bad. But when I went out to view the damage, I went all over looking at the devastation. I went to Pine Villa first. When I saw it, it was really unbelievable. I never thought the building would hold. It was facing so that the main building took most of the wind. I went on walking around. I thought that my part of the school was OK. Until we all went back to school on Thursday; the whole school went back. I went in some of the computer rooms. I screamed. I didn't scream when I saw my house, but when I saw that room, a $150,000 room full of brand-new Macintosh computers—brand-new, never been used, just gone, full of water and muck—I just screamed. I had been holding it in. I just had to let it out. I just couldn't believe it, so much damage. The new text books, everything, everything ruined.

New voice:

I felt that way when I saw my house. My house was totaled. I forgot about work at that point, about the kids. It's like I had to keep pinching myself to know that I was still here. And then once we got here to Porter, it's like an escape. I forget what's really there. But now going back and being in it again and trying to teach. Now, that's going to be really difficult.

New voice:

You know it's like being able to leave all of that behind, the memories of being in that house with the roof tearing off, being in the linen closet for all that long time with my husband and my son. . . . Coming here where it's air-conditioned and clean and pretty, I can put that behind me. It's like an escape, especially when people are telling you that it's going to be alright. But Monday. I have to relive it all again.

New voice:

That's what I'm afraid of.

New voice:

I feel that too.

New voice:

At first I didn't feel that. I thought that the most important thing was to get back to our school. The kids need some normalcy back in their life. And at least they'd get a meal, maybe more. For me, a way to escape from my problems was to go back to work and see the kids. I was worried about the kids. The best thing about coming to Porter was the warm welcome that we received. When that bus pulled up, the first bus, the look on those children's faces was so happy. You can imagine how they felt. They thought that the teachers were gone. They had left the school. The kids had to load the buses from Pine Villa and come to a place where they didn't think there would be anyone to know them. They thought they would get all new teachers. They were really scared. When they saw all the teachers outside waiting for them and Porter had a band, I mean the look on those children's faces was just happy. We were happy too because we got to see them!

New voice:

I had been down to Pine Villa since 7:30 in the morning and kids started arriving. The military were there and the Red Cross. When we tried to put them in line to get on the bus, they started crying. I'll never forget this. One boy yelled, "Please, Don't go. What if we can't find you!" I said, "Don't worry. I'll be there when you get off the bus. The first thing when he saw me when he got off the bus, he grabbed me.

New voice:

All the kids were so happy to be here. It was a really good feeling. They were happy, but they were also scared. They were silent when they got off because they were afraid of the unknown.

New voice:

For Mr. Zerlin and all of them to have such a really warm welcome, it was really touching. It was so nice. When the kids saw the welcome with the band and everything, they were amazed. They may have even thought, "Wow, this reception. What did we do to deserve this?" I'm not sure that they realized that Mr. Zerlin and his staff wanted us to feel welcome. We didn't know ourselves what to expect. That Friday before school started was the only time we had been here.

New voice:

Friday was the best. That day they had an elaborate program. People here at Porter walk around with a smile. They are friendly. I never met such friendly people. We introduced ourselves by grade group, then they sung us songs like "Getting to Know You" and "That's what Friends are For." I think that our faculty was still in shell shock because Porter had all this energy and they were glad that we were here. You could tell that. Our faculty was skeptical. The Porter people were always on the up. Why?

New voice:

I think that for many of the Pine Villa people, seeing the Porter people as always being up was disturbing. Some people have had a hard time dealing with all of this energy and enthusiasm and happiness. I even go through this myself; it depends on the time, the day, the mood. I think that a lot of people still had it in their mind that their classroom and their educational materials were destroyed. Many of them lost a lot, and here they see all of these people so up. What's wrong with them? Didn't they lose anything? I know that many of the Porter faculty lost their homes too. The majority lived here and had some damage, some more than others. But they were just smooth. And well, swell.

New voice:

When I came here, I was still in shock. They lifted me also. I didn't want to be lifted at first. I felt that they had a safe harbor. They had their school.

We lost a lot and we lost our school too. We had lost our home and we had lost our school. A lot of the teachers just didn't feel like they had the energy to come back; they just didn't feel like it. You lose your home; you lose your other love, your school. All the materials, everything. This is a major change! It's still hard to adjust. And the real kicker is . . . it's going to be even harder to adjust when we get back. We are going from one extreme to the other. Here nice and clean; go down there, we're going to have to clean like we're at home to make the place presentable. We're going to have to go back and remember and relive it all over again.

New voice:

Well, I think you have to get your mind set. It's not the end of the world. Other people have had disasters and lived through it. It's made me think about other things, the people in Africa who are starving and the kids in Yugoslavia who are being killed. And I have to say, well, it could have been like that for us. Things happen for a reason and they put things in perspective. You have to get your mind together and not dwell on the material things, like having a nice school. I think that we took a lot of things for granted. If we can make it through the year, we can handle anything. If we let us get us down, then we will always be beat.

New voice:

We have to be open minded and willing to accept change. Not have tunnel vision, and help each other, hug each other and hold on to each other. Hugs and kind words, they help. I think that our staff is strong enough to make it. You know, whether you want to live on life's terms, that is a fact that you have to accept. You can let it break you or make you. Life goes on. When you look at death right in the face, . . . when you do things, it's not always about self, not always just what you want.

New voice:

I've seen that we have grown closer. But we have to wait and see. I know there will be a lot of stressed-out people, and this experience, the next few weeks, are going to be difficult. The support of others has really helped being here; seeing the kids, being together has helped to take my mind off of everything at home.

New voice:

Seeing the smiles, the faces, knowing that things will get better. I know that I have to live one day at a time. I don't know what tomorrow will bring. One day at a time, acceptance. Some things you have to accept. It takes courage. Don't be part of the problem, be part of the solution.

New voice:

> I have to be patient. I have a job. I think something good will happen. Until Andrew, I was having the best year of my life. I'm still having a good year.

When asked how they saw the rebuilding of the community proceed after the storm and where they got the courage to go on, one of the teachers explained:

> The strength of our heritage comes from the church. The politicians usually go to the minister when they have a request, and if they agree, the ministers will relay the messages. The strength comes from the church. At Pine Villa, the coalition of churches has established this order—politicians, ministers, and people who work in the community, leaders that people look up to. People will come to hear leaders, like Jessie Jackson, because they will get inner strength by hearing the message from the messenger. Pine Villa is in this kind of neighborhood. It's just strength. It's not a whole lot of money.

New voice:

> I agree, but there's another aspect to it. Montessori is a magnet program that exists to reestablish the black-white ratio in the school. The coalition consists of those people who live in the community. But that's not the whole Pine Villa community. Pine Villa is also made up of a white region, the Redlands. There has to be another action beyond the cohesive areas right around the school because these other parents have chosen to send their children to this magnet school. We have to include the community or communities of these children too. There is not an immediate area church or coalition that represents this group of students.

New voice:

> What we are saying is the hurricane is not a black or white thing; our school is Pine Villa/Montessori. It is important that we stop dealing with each other as separate and deal with each other as one. . . . We are not two schools with one boss, and we must live life on life's terms. We have to face the fact that some of the parents have the capital; the majority of them have the capital; we may have the inner strength.

New voice:

> Not all of them have the capital.

New voice:

> Not all of them, but the majority. But we need to come together. It doesn't take Montessori to make Pine Villa. It doesn't take the Redlands Park to

make Pine Villa. We have to do it together. All the teachers and all of the students, so that we have some form of unity. That is the only way that we are going to make it at this time.

New voice:

Unity is going to come from both. Our school consists of a bigger picture. It's all the people. The principal can't make it. The superintendent can't fix it. But we, we, we can fix it. We have to come to the realization that this is where we are. Do we want to make some changes or do we want to stay complacent? That's the issue!

New voice:

And divided!

New voice:

Yes, and divided; that's the issue! And we have to deal with it with com-passion and passion! It takes two or more, to do it. To work together doesn't take anything away from anyone else. We have to look at the way things operate; check the motives. Self gain? When Hurricane Andrew went through, it went through everyone's house the same. We are all in it together. That's why I'm saying that some good should come out of this. I'm saying it's not a color thing, it's a people thing. Everybody has a story to tell. We have to accept people the way they are.

New voice:

This is like a new beginning. We are going to be starting all over again. Maybe that's the real story. Maybe we hadn't realized it but we may be coming to something new.

New voice:

That's the real story.

At this time an announcement over the loud speaker:

All Pine Villa equipment must be packed up immediately and sent to the Pine Villa office. All Pine Villa teachers must send their equipment to the office now. A custodian will be coming around to your room to issue you a sheet indicating that all of your equipment has been sent to the office.

With this final announcement, the teachers moved to finish packing. We agreed to meet with them the following Friday to see how the move had gone.

のめる

Although we were never formally introduced to the faculty at Pine Villa, word spread throughout the school about our interest in documenting the rebuilding process. When we arrived at Pine Villa on the following Friday (October 23, 1992), teachers with whom we had not previously spoken saw us and initiated conversations in the hallways. One teacher who was eager to share her insights made the following observation:

> One thing that I've noticed about the faculty and staff is how happy they are to be back here. It's really a comforting thing for them to be back. It's like returning some part of their life to normal. The move was very difficult. It required a lot of adjustment for people who were already required to make adjustments. Something in our lives has returned to normal again. Some have lost their cars, their homes; some are not even living with their families now, but at least the school is one place that is beginning to come back to normal for them. They can relate to the kids and the adults. It was a very difficult move for all of us. The kids didn't know where they were. Most of these kids don't get out of their own neighborhood. Here they were going to some place where they didn't have any reference to in terms of time or distance. It was bewildering for them. Coming back here makes them feel comfortable. They are back home.[3]

Another teacher shared his thoughts about the move as we chatted on the playground:

> This will be the third change since we have started school this year. . . . Kids have been moved from one class to another, and now they are going to move them to another. I coordinated the bus transportation between here and Porter. I'd get here early in the morning and coordinate the transportation and then come back here at night and meet them when they returned.

In describing the community, he observed:

> There are a lot of teachers who have taught here a long time, maybe twenty-five years. They know the mothers and grandmothers of the children. A lot of the teachers live in this area. They got devastated. I was just talking to a friend who lives right by the trailer park where the eight people got killed. She stayed in the storm by herself. Parts of people's trailers were going through the house. She spent the night in the garage. The librarian had to take a leave of absence for a year. Her entire structure where she lived and everything she owned was damaged. She had to move back to Ohio. A lot of people were really hard hit in this area. Most of these kids here are from the HUD housing project. They are awarding

bids to contract that out; now a lot of the people are living in trailer city up the street. This area used to be a beautiful park. But now its a trailer park; FEMA has installed electricity and plumbing. The HUD project is really going to need major repairs. Most of these children and the Mays Middle School kids are living in the FEMA trailers. They are beautiful trailers. They've also been given vouchers by the Red Cross. There is still a soup kitchen over there. There are a lot of things that we can't do right now because there are no fences. No major equipment was left standing. The hurricane knocked down all of our equipment. We will gradually try to replace it. It is very important to get this fenced in because the people from the neighborhood see this as a line of demarcation and they don't come in. It establishes lines of communication. It also promotes communication with the kids. We always tell them they can't go outside the fence. A kid gets mad—he may try and run home. They don't have to run very far. It's a touchy situation without our fences up. We need the fences up. We need our walkie-talkies back.

When asked specifically about the move, the teacher said:

You know everybody resists change—having to learn new procedures, new administrative requirements in a new organization. Most people take the path of least resistance. I figure that it would have been better for everybody if they had just knocked down the structures that they had; they were already in the process of redoing a lot. They had the federal money. They should have just gone on ahead with the major building program that they had planned. They stopped because of the static of the faculty at the other school. They weren't in control. You feel like you're a secondhand citizen. I never felt that way. I thought the people at Porter were really great. Really neat. I think it is more of a "being in charge" kind of thing. When you are in someone else's school, it's like your borrowing their things. I guess that some of the teachers did resent being at Porter. I enjoyed it. The facilities where we were were gorgeous.

Although we had made arrangements to meet with the same group of teachers with whom we had talked the previous week, the second meeting was limited. Everyone seemed to want to get on with their work. Many of the teachers' feelings were upbeat now that they were back. Typical were the following comments:

I remember that I said that I was afraid of the unknown. When I walked in, I was totally surprised. It wasn't what I had felt before. Everybody was running around trying to help everyone. It was different. It was like, "Yes, you can. You know you can!" It made me feel good. It relieved some

pressure and some anxiety. My husband said to me, "Why are you antici-
pating destruction? You have to be very positive." When I first thought
about coming back, it was just like reliving the destruction all over again.
I came here the day after the storm. I was here after the storm. I saw the
children. I saw the mothers. I saw them crying.[4]

New Voice:

> If we had stayed at Porter longer, it would have been easier. I have mixed
> emotions. As much as possible, the school has been cleaned, and it isn't as
> bad as we had anticipated. I still feel that we should had stayed at Porter. I
> got comfortable there. It was safe. If we had stayed there, maybe we would
> have had something different to come back to. I think that if we had stayed
> there longer, when we came back all of the teachers would have had their
> own rooms, which they don't at this time. Other things would have been
> together that we are putting together now. We are all working very hard.
> We would have come to something more formed. They are still cleaning
> out the damp and damaged things.

New Voice:

> I have mixed emotions. I would have liked to have stayed at Porter. I still
> have some mixed emotions talking to some of the teachers and the chil-
> dren. It's almost like some pressure has been released. The teachers want
> their own books. They don't have to say, "I can't touch that." The teachers
> are feeling more responsibility for things here. Before, there was someone
> else to put the blame on. Now, it's like, "Let's wake up!"

New Voice:

> It was a realization that the school was the top of the line that bothered
> some of us. They have a lot of flexible space, a lot of new equipment,
> and they have a lot to say about what education is all about.

New Voice:

> I am right back home. Our things were damaged or stolen. It's not that we
> need all the material things, but they really look good. Here, we're going to
> make this look good. We're getting materials from everywhere; people
> are very generous. I'm not worried about that. I'm glad to get back. Here,
> I can see my friend. I can see that she's alright and she can see that I am
> alright. I know where she's going and she knows where I'm going. We can
> reach out and touch each other. It's like where you're at home, you drop
> your shoes. You know where they are and you can go back and pick up
> your shoes.

New Voice:

> I think that it is still a mess here. We could have had much more if we had just waited. Look at this place and look at theirs. Each teacher there had a workroom. It was wonderful. I think that we could have had something like that. Coming back here this early, maybe it was right, maybe not.

New Voice:

> Our children and we deserve a lot more. I want the top of the line for our children. I want air-conditioning in the cafeteria like they have. The rooms have carpeting. The bathrooms are in the rooms so the children don't get wet. You can control them and be safe.

Our meeting was of necessity limited and circumscribed. It was clear that the above quotes reflect the general tone of the teachers on their return. The teachers and the administrators were busy going about the business of building a school and an educational program and did not need us as researchers distracting them from their work. We decided to temporarily suspend our interviews. Although we returned several times to observe and talk briefly in the hallways, we did not attempt to conduct any more interviews until the end of the school year.

Reflecting on the schools we had been observing, we realized that at Ashe and Porter the beginning of the school year was unambiguously positive. Once school started and everyone had a chance to get back in touch with each other, the year moved forward. It was a difficult year in terms of the absences and the stress that had to be overcome or at least dealt with. But it was a solid move forward.

Nothing about Pine Villa beginning the school year was as clear as at either Ashe or Porter. For Pine Villa, there were three beginnings; one at Pine Villa, the second at Porter, and the third back at Pine Villa. The faculty had mixed feelings and thoughts about all of these changes. The physical aspects of the moves—the sorting, cleaning, packing, and unpacking—were taxing. Some of the faculty were happy to be at Porter, even if they had to share the facilities. Others thought it was important to have their own space—their own school. When the teachers returned to Pine Villa, they were glad to be back. Then as they looked around, they wondered, "We're back, but back to what?

PINE VILLA AT THE END OF THE SCHOOL YEAR

Although we visited the school several times during the year, it was not until the end of the 1993 school year that we returned once again to interview the teachers at Pine Villa. Traveling to Pine Villa from Porter at the beginning of June—now nine months after the hurricane—still provided us with a keen sense of the destruction that had occurred. Leaving Kendall Drive and heading south toward the Florida Turnpike, the houses along the sides of the road appeared to be more damaged and less restored than in the area around Kendall. The farther along the Turnpike we drove, the more visible the damage became. We were returning to the area that had experienced the main force of the storm. Here the roofs were still either severely damaged with exposed gray beams and collapsed walls or completely restored and new. Graffiti was written on almost every fence and on many of the walls of the unrestored homes. The graffiti had replaced the "We survived the hurricane!" signs seen spray painted all around the area right after the storm. The sprawling writing, as well as the unkempt appearance of the neighborhoods, was in sharp contrast to the modest but well-kept appearance of this area prior to the hurricane. The area could be described as having a third world quality. A great deal of debris still remained uncollected. Huge piles of trash, cars, old furniture, and debris from destroyed homes were visible throughout.

Evidence of the storm could be seen everywhere. There were few standing trees. Many of the trees that did remain upright appeared sick or dead. Homes, large multistory buildings, motels, housing complexes, and complete shopping malls had not yet been repaired. We were surrounded by shells of structures with roofs and walls caved in and parking lots full of rubble and trash.

Many businesses had left the area. Those few businesses that were open were freshly painted and often displayed flags showing that they were ready to serve customers. Typically, these were fast food restaurants, gas stations, and car parts stores. The return of a few restaurants meant that food was at least available. Because most of the large grocery and other retail stores had not yet reopened in the area, people still had to drive long distances to obtain basic supplies. Cutler Ridge Shopping Center—the main mall in the area—was not rescheduled to reopen until March 1994, although a restaurant and a retail chain store in the center were open for business. The need for transportation posed a real difficulty for many of the people whose cars and trucks had been damaged by the hurricane. With the disappearance of the business community, people with already restricted budgets now had to spend funds for taxis or, at the very least, pay neighbors for gas to take them shopping. When we returned to Pine Villa in early June, the parking lot was full of cars. Many people were still living in the FEMA trailer park adjacent to the school. Dade County Public School work trucks were pulled up near the buildings. Workmen were on the roofs and around the buildings still making repairs. There were several signs of progress: the first was the absence of the demolished, transportable structure that had once housed the computer labs, the assistant principal's office, and the classrooms in the front of the school and the second was the presence of a new fence surrounding the school yard.

Melvin Denis, the school's principal, had provided us a great deal of information throughout the school year. The closing of the year, while perhaps a welcome event, brought a new and difficult responsibility for him—the task of telling several of his teachers that they would no longer be employed at the school following the hurricane because of the decline in student enrollment. Saying good-bye to people with whom you have worked closely is never easy. Losing people with whom you have formed a bond of collaboration as a result of adversity is even more difficult. Both Denis and Joanne Lasky, the assistant principal, discussed the release of the Pine Villa teachers. As Denis explained the situation:

> I am going to lose at least seven teachers, maybe eight. I'm right now in the process of preparing a surplus list. Our enrollment didn't go back up to where we thought it would be. It's a little over 750; we were around 1,100 for the elementary school. We've had to make some adjustments. I've got to meet with people today and let them know that they don't have a job here. I felt so bad on Thursday when we got the news. While the reduction will effect the school, it will not impact on the magnet aspect of the school, the Montessori program.[5]

According to Denis:

> We did the preliminary effort at job reduction this past week. We could loose additional teachers if the enrollment goes down further. We have sent our surveys to our families through our students, and letters to the parents who were in the magnet program wanting to know if they were going to be coming back in the fall. Some parents indicated that they would. (Denis Interview)

Denis talked about the criteria for making the decisions on which of the teachers would be surplused the following year:

> In making the decisions about who will be surplused, we have to look at years of service, whether they were a tenured or nontenured teachers, primary or intermediate, and their programs. Some are in federal programs. What is curious about the whole thing is that some of the people have like twelve years of service and are going to be surplused. Our magnet program has the priority. People in that program have specialized training. I've had to work with personnel downtown and the unions to see whether or not the personnel in the specialized programs can be pushed through to allow us to keep those people. A lot of the people in the magnet program are beginning teachers, or second or third year teachers. Those are the lower teachers on the list, in terms of tenure, but since the district put a lot of money into training these teachers, we going to have to establish some type of waver or exception so that we don't include those people in the process, or it won't be a magnet anymore. (Denis Interview)

Lasky explained:

> Our classroom teachers in one program are as good as the teachers in another program. One has been here two years, but she really bonded with the children. This teacher was down here after the storm looking after the children that she knew, trying to care for them and take care of them. She had damage to her own home, but she cared so much for these children that she came here. We don't want to loose her; she's the type of teacher that we really need.[6]

Hurricane Andrew worked in many subtle ways to affect the perceptions of the teachers and students at Porter. For example, when Pine Villa was paired with Porter at the beginning of the school year, both the teachers and the students had a whole new set of experiences to assimilate that went beyond just the issue of the destruction caused by the hurricane. The teachers and students at Pine Villa had to address the disparity between Porter's bright, modern, well-equipped school plant with its middle-class suburban environment and the reality of their own school's condition with its lack of modern conveniences such as air-conditioning and teacher workrooms. More importantly, it had to address the poverty and lack of resources in the greater Goulds community that made the recovery from the hurricane even more difficult than in other parts of the county.

Hurricane Andrew did not bring about these disparities. It did however highlight them. What Hurricane Andrew did was exacerbate an already difficult situation and make the process of creating a positive learning environment even more difficult.

ASSESSING THE IMPACT
OF THE HURRICANE AT PINE VILLA

One of the teachers remarked to us that many of the children at the school believed that only children, not faculty, were hurt by the hurricane. Just how badly the school personnel were affected by the storm is indicated by the results of a survey conducted by the researchers during the last week of the 1992-93 school year. Of the sixty-two potential faculty respondents, fifty-six or 90 percent responded to the survey. Of those responding, only four, or 7 percent of the faculty indicated that they had no major damage to their homes. Fifty-two faculty reported sustaining major damage. Thirty-one of these, or 60 percent, indicated they were able to remain living in their houses after the storm. Many people selected to live in their homes instead of moving so that they could closely supervise repairs and prevent potential theft or looting. Often remaining in the home meant incredible difficulties and inconveniences as whole walls, roofs, and floors were repaired. Of the twenty-one educators who had to leave their homes, only nine, or 43 percent, were unable to move back into their homes as of mid-June 1993, almost a year later. Two of these indicated that they would never move back. In terms of the length of time required to complete home repairs, one individual reported repairs were completed by September 1992, eight by the end of December 1992, and four by March 1993. Five anticipated completion by the end of June, twenty by the end of the summer, seven by the end of 1994, and one after the end of 1994. As the survey indicated, the faculty at Pine Villa found themselves coping with repairs and rebuilding at home and at school. While many were somewhat optimistic about the rebuilding, as the year progressed the optimism drained away leaving the harsh reality of a highly stressed and vulnerable group.

Because of the severe damage that had occurred to the Pine Villa buildings, significant repairs continued to be made at the school as the year progressed. These repairs could not wait until summer. Many students and faculty members, besides having to endure the inevitable noise, dust, and confusion that accompanies a rebuilding, became ill from exposure to caustic chemicals used in the renovations at Pine Villa. Sick teachers were unable to come to work. Sick children created extra burdens. The difficulties continued to mount with each month of the rebuilding process until the whole school began to wonder if they would literally be able to complete the school year, much less put their lives in order again.

Instead of soliciting the assistance of substitutes who were not available as readily as in other schools in the county, Pine Villa had to depend on shifting around teachers and students in the school to cover for people when they were ill or away from school doing hurricane related recovery tasks. It was not surprising that, faced with the difficulties imposed by working at an old and damaged school located in the center of the hurricane destruction area, some of the faculty perceived their experience during the 1992-93 school year as a series of inequities.

How the teachers at Pine Villa coped with the challenges presented to them in the year following the hurricane can be seen in our conversations with one of the most vocal and insightful of the teachers we had first spoken to in the fall. When we first met her in the fall, she appeared energetic and enthusiastic. Now, in early June, she seemed tired and somewhat older. Her face and voice had a mystical quality, as though she had seen a vision. Always friendly and outgoing, when she sat down with us, she began to summarize her experiences somewhat hesitantly: "We are still recovering. It's been very hard. I don't think personally that everything has been recovered. We are still learning to live life on life's terms."

Learning to live life on life's terms, we realized, was a theme that summarized the thoughts of many of the teachers at Pine Villa. Living on life's terms could be considered as a way of dealing with life at Pine Villa. There was no way to gain control, to establish a consistent pattern of recovery. One had to take what came if one were to survive. For this teacher, and probably many others, accepting life as it came was an important survival strategy, a way of looking at the world.

> Some times have been harder than others. One thing that I have learned from this ordeal—I value life. I don't value things; I value life. I learned that in this form of recovery, I must enjoy the moment, to live in the moment, and to take time for myself. Take time for my family. I am a workaholic. I enjoy working, but now I'm learning more and more to keep something back for myself. I can't be all things to all people. My stress level has dropped because of my new attitude. I used to be a real go-getter; I still am, but I've learned to manage. I learned to manage rather than to do everything and to be everything to all people. I think that Hurricane Andrew, in looking at the positive side, gave me a different outlook on life. It showed me exactly what I needed and what I can do without. A lot of things . . . have happened to me, to my family, to my colleagues since Andrew. This too shall pass. Some people lost family. Some people have

had trouble, as we all know, with contractors. Sometimes we have to cry on each other. Some of us have had things taken from us because of the "haves" and the "have nots" in our society. We have come to the point where we lift each other up. When you feel bad, there is always someone there to pat us on the back, to learn to rely on each other. The tolerance level is not great, but someone is there to tolerate it for you. Someone is there to carry us through.[7]

As she reflected, she began to provide a summary of the year's experiences. As she did so, the statistics and the lists of storm consequences took on new meaning:

We've had a lot to endure. The children, the children, for example, have not been as calm. You remember what I was saying about tolerance. I may go in and take a teacher's class and let that teacher have a breather; you know sometimes you just have to get away from it so you can have a better outlook, a better perspective on what you are about and what your purpose is. I found teachers have come to know each other better. There may have been someone in the school that you didn't know before. You know them now because we have had to share. Everybody has a story; everybody has their own horror story. Teachers have had to go to the doctor. They are sick and now they are putting on a new roof. We wonder, when will it end? When will it end? So you are forced even more than ever to live on life's terms, and value life, even when you don't want to. We still have emotions. We are still very emotional. We are very emotional. That's why I can't say to you one particular thing that has happened, but I can give you, in an around circle, that we are emotional!

Like many others who work at Pine Villa, this teacher had a strong conviction about her reasons for being a teacher and for working at the school:

I come to work because I want to be here. There is no check in the world that can pay me to come here. I come here because of the love for children, the love of the community, and because I am from where they come from. I was born in the ghetto. I believe that as someone helped my father, and my father helped me, I am obligated, I am committed to help someone else. That is my true purpose and my compass. I never forget. I have taught in many schools, but the greatest gift and satisfaction is knowing that someone needed me in an inner city school, because I was going back home. My grandmother told me, "You can't keep what you have unless you give it back." I can't keep what I have unless I give it back. That's my purpose. I can't be all that I want to be; I am still not all that I want to be; I want a Ph.D. in psychology. I tell the little children around me that I have dreams, that I still have dreams. Dreams are not only for dreamers; dreams are for doers. It can happen. It has happened to me. My life has not always been a bed of roses. It still isn't, but I want to let them know that they can rise above it.

Observations of the disparities between the newly built Porter and the older more established Pine Villa came to the surface as this teacher discussed her perceptions of inequalities and the need for change:

> Here you have to do what you have to do. We don't have what we want; we have to fight every step of the way. We are like an inner city school. We can easily be overlooked. One of the teachers went to the school board. We've had promises before the hurricane. Things escalate. It's like a pimple. It gets hot and it gets hot and it becomes a boil. It's ready to explode. Hurricane Andrew just exploded the boil. It's hot everywhere here. You go somewhere else and it's not hot. Let's face it. We have to fight every step of the way. And we have to come to work and help these kids. It's like an onion. The onion skin comes off. What I may have been able to take yesterday, I can no longer take today. What was acceptable then, or that I may have tolerated then, the same conditions that are no longer acceptable to me, I think that people fool themselves. I think that in this society, people don't want to hear the real thing; people don't want to hear the truth. They don't want to hear from a person like me because I am going to call a spade a spade. I come from the soul of the soul, and they buy our people every day. I will be the one they won't buy because I am teaching children every day that "The dope giver will buy you; society will buy you. I know. I have been there. You don't have to have a fight. Live life on life's terms, in the principle of life, and make your own way and be your own boss." I teach children to be their own boss, to make their own choices, and to suffer the consequences. I can't blame you, but take your foot off of me. Take your foot off of me!

When asked about the effects of the hurricane in terms of perceptions of the recovery process and the rebuilding of Pine Villa, the teacher related:

> The hurricane has revealed things that for whatever reason, people may not have wanted to acknowledge. What I could tolerate then, I can't tolerate today. It's unacceptable. It's not negotiable. You can take children and you can show them the best in the world; you can show teachers the top of the line equipment. You mean to tell me that you think they don't want that too? You can show teachers the state of the art, everything that they could want, and you mean to tell me that I don't want that too? You can tell me that I can be cool in one school, but I got to come home to the other school

and be hot in an oven? You think I don't feel the difference? You can tell me that I can have lavish lunches and I have to come here and have something prepared somewhere else? We're proud people. People here are proud, be it Black, be it Spanish, be it White. We don't look at color here. We don't have time for that. We don't have room for it. It's education that we're here for.

Later, the same teacher summarized her thoughts on the experiences of the year following the hurricane in the following way:

Andrew opened many eyes: the children, the parents, teachers, and the community. Gilbert Porter, the school of the 1990s; Pine Villa, the school of the 1950s: they looked different, even smelled different. We love the differences! However, when you have to return to the reality of it all, resentments, angry feelings appear and no success arises. Education is the key to success. Give us a better environment, give us hope and share the wealth of society. Validate our feelings. Don't tell us to go away. People must deal with the pimple now. We must make the inner city an asset, not a liability.

As part of our interviews in early June, Joanne Lasky, the assistant principal at Pine Villa, met with us in a tiny room in the library that served as her office. A teacher was also with Lasky for the interview—participating in but not formally part of the interview. Lasky began to summarize the recovery efforts by saying:

People need to study the recovery effort. I was noticing the bumper sticker that says, "We survived the hurricane, but the recovery is hell." Let me tell you. It's worse! I personally don't feel that I have been able to do half of what I had planned to do, what I needed to do, and yet I have been busier, worked harder, this year than I ever had in my life. If there could have been four of me in my position, maybe we could see some daylight. If I had not had the support of teachers like the ones here, I don't know what I would have done. They winged it. We all have had to wing it.[8]

Lasky made it clear that she would not, could not, relive the experience of the past year again. As she recollected:

I was a teacher here in 1975 and got surplused, just like the teachers are experiencing this week. I have always been involved in Chapter I schools. I think that many administrators and teachers care about communities such as this one. People don't work in a community that has low-achieving children, people living at poverty level way below standard, and educational problems unless they are dedicated to making a difference. I had the opportunity four years ago to come back here as an administrator. I wouldn't relive this year again. I simply do not have the strength to face another hurricane. It was like watching the hurricane movie on television. I kept saying, "You're missing it. It's much more." The story centered on three or four families, which I understand that they had to do. But when they had an opportunity to show the thirty or forty miles of devastation, they showed patches. (Lasky Interview)

Lasky underscored what many others had said, "You can't really imagine how all encompassing the devastation has been here." Almost everyone with whom we talked expressed the sense of devastation that Lasky emphasized:

There's no real way to communicate the sense of desolation. I don't think the television programs have showed the magnitude of what happened. Maybe you had to live it. Perhaps the best that could be done is an hour of before and after shots. If someone documented it. I didn't get power for almost a week so I don't know what was on TV. I still wonder. It's like I lost a part of my life. We bought a place in North Carolina this spring. I'm not going to be here to go through this again. (Lasky Interview)

Lasky had been very helpful throughout the year, providing us with information and directing us to other helpful sources. In our final interview, she reemphasized the need and the importance of studying the recovery from a disaster:

We need to have people study the rebuilding process so we can be better prepared in the future. [We need it] for every county that is in danger of a disaster, that could be pretty much anyone, because you could have a fire do what the storm did here. There needs to be a plan, a procedure. I just got a memo entitled, "Reporting of Donated Products in Excess of $400." Several years ago, we worked very hard to earn six to eight Publix computers. But they weren't on an inventory. We knew that we had them. But there was no particular place to put them in our records because they were donated. Our Chapter I inventory. We had a copy in the main office and our Chapter I office had a copy. Both offices were wiped out. We don't know exactly what we had. We were required to say how many tape recorders we had. With all of our records damaged, we don't know exactly how many tape recorders we had. The task has been incredible, and there was no procedure, not one, that covers everything. I sometimes have nightmares about being caught committing fraud. I wonder, "Did I put this computer on two different lists? Am I going to get paid for it twice?" Is someone going to come and point their finger at me and say, "You didn't have two. You only had one." I am sure that the teachers will tell you that we were making lists at Porter when the Army came in and decided, "This looks wet," and pitched it out. Picture the living room in your house, the way you left it this morning. I bet you, if you had to make a list of everything in that room, just that one room, that you would leave things out. And we had to make lists of everything in a whole school. (Lasky Interview)

Helping each other—pulling together—was critical to people. Lasky emphasized how:

We've helped each other, hugged each other, picked up and caught each other. I don't see that we have any end of it. I don't think that we have scratched the surface. We may have finished with the things that we lost, but now new things are coming in. I don't have any place to put them. There is no place to put the new textbooks. I lost sixteen classrooms. When I say I, I mean the school. They gave us three back. We also lost students. However, do I order textbooks for all sixteen classes because the FEMA money is there. What do you do with the books for sixteen classrooms if you don't have one extra space? The assistant principal's office is in a library closet. Resource teachers are in a bookroom that is filled, and where do you put the new texts? And if I don't order them, am I responsible to the children who don't have the books? The answers are not there. There is no single person who can give you a specific answer to anything. We need to have a way to plan on a larger scale than just going from one crisis solution to another. And yet, because we have never undergone this experience before, no one had any real idea what to do or to anticipate. (Lasky Interview)

The rebuilding of the library or media center had been a major concern all year. It was hoped, initially, that a whole new school could be rebuilt for Pine Villa. While that was not going to be possible, Lasky did have several positive pieces information to share:

Because we were so destroyed, and because we did have plans and because the eight classroom transportable building was completely destroyed, they are going to build a completely new up-to-date media center. It won't give us back the eight classrooms, but it will give us the technology and resource center that we need. So that is the good news that came out of the storm. They anticipate that they will break ground in September. However, with everything backlogged, that's just the anticipated date. I don't have an end date. (Lasky Interview)

Another positive piece of news concerned a recent grant:

We did get a grant. I wrote a grant proposal requesting $11,000 for school uniforms. We did get $11,000 in uniforms from the Hurricane Relief Fund for

Dade County Public Schools. We didn't want people's old unwashed clothes. What we did with all of that stuff that we received was put it out on tables on two Saturdays and let the community come and pick things that they needed. We boxed the rest up and gave it to the Salvation Army. Our students want to look good just like everybody else's children. (Lasky Interview)

In our interviews with administrators such as Lasky, there was a general consensus that the school system's central administration had done an excellent job in leading the recovery. Lasky reflected the thoughts of many others when she said, "I think that Mr. Denis, Mr. Visiedo, and the regional superintendents worked selflessly. I know how hard they worked. We all have. But no one had a disaster plan. No one knew what to do. We're not blaming anyone. We all have worked to make this year a success." (Lasky Interview)

The teacher sitting in on the interview, however, reflected a different perspective. She indicated that in her opinion, the district did not provide enough support or the right kind of support. She argued, "From a teacher's standpoint, we need compassion. We need to be validated. We know it's our problem, but it's also their problem."[9]

One important way that the school district did support the schools was through the use of FEMA funds to employ the same number of teachers as the previous year—even though the school had a lower enrollment. Administrators were permitted to use these teachers in any way that they wished. Lasky explained:

They gave us what the district called "FEMA packs"; eight of our teachers and some of our security guards were paid for by FEMA, based on our enrollment from last year. Our student-teacher ratio was very low this year based on the FEMA packs, except for one grade. That grade is still low in comparison to the county average, but it is higher than other grades. For example, I have kindergarten classes with eighteen. That's a teacher's dream. Without the FEMA packs, we would have had to make the classes larger and release some of the teachers because there wasn't the enrollment this year that we had last year. We felt that it was a wonderful opportunity for the teachers to have small classes. We have those extra teachers. We could have pulled them and used them as substitutes, but that would not have necessarily benefitted the students, it would have benefitted the teachers but not the students. We had to make that choice. The district left it up to us. We chose to lower the primary teachers' class size. While the district really did help us, we could have used more, both in the planning and decision making process and in ways to receive additional support, substitutes, and workers to help sort through and respond to the paperwork. (Anonymous Teacher Interview)

The need for a well-thought-out disaster plan was a consistent point with all the school administrators interviewed. No one wanted to be critical, but everyone felt the need to be better prepared. Lasky stated the importance of a plan, again, in reflecting on the year, this time in terms of the union:

> The union has been supportive in a lot of ways. I happen to know that the representative for our region spoke on behalf of Pine Villa and requested assistance. I don't think the union had a plan either. I don't want to criticize the union. They just didn't have a plan. I believe they will now—just like at your house. I had my windows boarded, but the boards came off. Now, I have the windows drilled, and I know what to do. (Anonymous Teacher Interview)

It's always difficult to make comparisons among schools. There are so many unseen and unaccounted for variables that can make a difference. At Pine Villa we heard many complaints about the difficult circumstances the year had presented. None of these complaints, however, appeared to be related to the proliferation of new educational innovations as was the case at Ashe and Porter.

In keeping with Project Phoenix, the school had submitted a proposal for becoming a resource center to provide increased community services. This was seen as being of particular importance to Pine Villa's principal Melvin Denis:

> I think that it's important to get all of our services together in one location. At the beginning of the year a lot of the agencies were in our building. That helped out tremendously, not only the school, but also the community. Having the agencies in the same central location helped the people without transportation quite a bit. When we send someone somewhere and when they get there, they find that it's not there; that's frustrating. Knowing how to go about getting there and having people there who can provide assistance helped out a lot. Some of the agencies even brought in surveys that we passed out to the families through the kids, to find out what were some of the things that people needed, what information they needed. I think that the schools played an important role in getting additional support.[10]

In order to ensure that the school would continue to provide support to the children and community, the Goulds Coalition—which existed before the hurricane—became an active voice for the school and the local area. As Lasky explained:

While the Coalition had been functioning before the storm, they have been very active after the storm. They, along with some of the PTA and community members, went to the school board. They had two concerns: one, that the general construction of the buildings in school should go forward; and two, that the school should be safe for the students and teachers. Just because the visible debris has been removed after the storm, the coalition is still concerned that the buildings are still unsafe.[11]

The coalition had worked with Pine Villa to establish a community resource center in a trailer to be located at the school. According to Lasky:

> We have applied for a grant to be able to provide more community services. All that is needed is a trailer which we believe that FEMA will purchase. Then the health department will locate a nurse in the trailer, and the police department will supply an officer who will be there as a truant and community officer. This will not be a full-service program but will be more than what most schools currently have in terms of community interaction. (Lasky Interview)

In all of the information shared during the interviews at the end of the 1992-93 school year at Pine Villa, a sense of general frustration came through most clearly—one expressed in many different ways. As one of the teachers explained: "There is a feeling here, and I understand it, that nothing has been done. There's a terrible sense of frustration. We're tired, very tired. But there's a difference between here, and say, the University of Miami. When you go there, you don't have the feeling of tiredness you have when you come here. We just can't get away from it."[12]

A feeling of tiredness is not surprising at the end of the school year. In schools across the county, students, teachers, and administrators expressed feelings of relief about and anticipation of the summer recess as well as tiredness for the academic year. These feelings were shared by the faculty at Pine Villa. Yet, the feelings here were also very different from what might be considered normal or typical. In schools all over the southern part of Dade County, people had passed beyond the concept of being tired. They were worn out from the constant daily struggle to put things anew, to return to normal, and to deal with complex and demanding situations.

Much of the frustration and exhaustion experienced by the teachers was clearly rooted not just in the hurricane but also in problems that were more deeply based in the community. In many communities the rebuilding process moved forward more easily than in Goulds and the area around Pine Villa because, while there were looters and threats of looting everywhere, most looters did not take and destroy things in the communities where they lived. This was not the case in the neighborhood surrounding Pine Villa. At Pine Villa, many of those responsible for looting following the storm lived near the school. For the teachers and the staff it was very intimidating to realize that these looters were there long after the storm was over. The threat of violence, encouraged by the hurricane, made the community seem just that much more unsafe and unsure.

CONCLUSION

The undercurrent of tension that existed when the Pine Villa faculty and students shared classrooms and facilities with Porter for the first month of school happened for many reasons. While the aftershock and the anguish the adults and children experienced was very real, there may have other factors that caused the faculty to be stressed. The desire that many of the Pine Villa faculty expressed to have a modern school, fully equipped with materials and resources, also weighed on the adults who knew that within a short period of time they would be returning to a very different type of school. Observing a community that supported the school's efforts by bringing in additional resources and serving as volunteers to ensure that the needs of teachers and students were met may also have been a collaborative process that was very different from what the Pine Villa faculty had previously experienced. Ultimately, these experiences provided the impetus for the Pine Villa teachers, administrators, PTA, and the Goulds Coalition to become committed to the development of the school within the community. Hurricane Andrew, in the end, simply emphasized the reality and problems that were already there and created a need to become more emphatic in addressing the problems of this reality.

A fundamental difference has always existed between the schools and communities of the "haves" and the "have nots." The difference does not simply lie in the numbers of dedicated teachers, capable leadership, or reasonable financial resources. Pine Villa had all of these. Instead the difference lies in the ways that these resources are organized and used and the ways that the school and community interface to appropriate and utilize these resources to effectively instruct the children.

Part of the appeal of Ashe and Porter, with their new buildings, multiple resource rooms, and special community activities, was the possibilities that these resources offered for building and extending the community. This need for community, which was equally as important in Pine Villa as it was in Ashe and Porter, was stifled by many other forces. Violence, threats of violence, and a sense of danger were only one part of the picture. The decay, the mold, and the odors that lurked within the closets, behind the classroom walls, and in the structures of the school also promoted a sense of fear and potential illness. The school was not safe from without or from within. How could the teachers and the administrators expect to rebuild? How could a sense of community be established here? These questions, although not always voiced by teachers and administrators, were clearly there as we contemplated Pine Villa's experience following the hurricane.

The efforts of the PTA, the Goulds Coalition, and the Project Phoenix proposal all provide evidence that like the royal poincianas that began blooming slowly, the environment within and around the school was seeking to develop and flower, in spite of many very real obstacles. Out of the natural disaster, there was a desire and a drive for rebirth. When all efforts are considered, it may be that the role of Pine Villa in contributing to the rebuilding of the Goulds community equaled, if not surpassed, that of many other schools that were less damaged. Pine Villa had a torn and shattered physical plant, few remaining resources, and many obstacles to be overcome. But the school provided the rallying point for the positive forces seeking promote the concept of the school within the community.

NOTES

1. Glenn R. Steinberg, "Teacher, Pine Villa Elementary School," *Miami Herald*, September 19, 1992, p. 22A.

2. Group interview with Pine Villa elementary teachers, October 16, 1994, conducted by Sandra H. Fradd. The following quotes in the text are from this interview. The individual quotes will not be cited in the text.

3. Interviews with Pine Villa teachers conducted October 23, 1993 with Sandra H. Fradd.

4. Interviews with Pine Villa teachers conducted October 23, 1993 with Sandra H. Fradd.

5. Interview with Melvin Denis conducted by Eugene F. Provenzo, Jr., May 1993, Miami, Florida. The following quotes in the text are from this interview. They are cited in the text.

6. Interview with Joanne Lasky conducted by Sandra H. Fradd and Eugene F. Provenzo, Jr., May 1993, Miami, Florida.

7. Interview with Pine Villa Elementary Teacher conducted by Sandra H. Fradd and Eugene F. Provenzo, Jr., May 1992, Miami, Florida. The following quotes in the text are from this interview. The individual quotes will not be cited in the text.

8. Lasky interview, *op. cit.*

9. Interview with Pine Villa Elementary teacher conducted by Sandra H. Fradd and Eugene F. Provenzo, Jr., May 1993, Miami, Florida. The following quotes in the text are from this interview. They are cited in the text.

10. Interview with Melvin Denis, *op. cit.*

11. Interview with Lasky, *op. cit.*

12. Interview with Pine Villa Elementary teacher conducted by Sandra H. Fradd and Eugene F. Provenzo, Jr., May 1993, Miami, Florida.

8
Conclusion

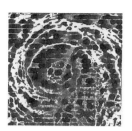

As the 1992-93 school year came to a close, the students and teachers at Ashe, Porter, and Pine Villa were exhausted, as were their counterparts in other schools across the county. The 1992-93 school year had been like no other. Yet, despite the turmoil and trouble, it had been a year in which people had gained new strengths and insights. Often these insights were more felt than clearly articulated. Sometimes they arose in discussions, such as the ones held by graduating seniors who attended a school highly impacted by the storm. Michelle Burman, for example, co-editor of the *Southernaire*, the year book for South Dade High School wrote:

> We are becoming more aware of the world surrounding us. Before, where we used to waste, now we reuse; where we were used to destroying, now we save. . . . We realize that we cannot treat this world as if it would be here forever. . . . Now the effort and the cause have become part of us like we never imagined. Here, in our homes, we see the destruction—and the repair. We know how important our trees and plants are, because we lost them. We learned that we must think and live differently, if we are to flourish again.[1]

Elinor Brecher, a *Miami Herald* staff writer who visited South Dade High School at the close of the school year to observe the effects of the storm during the closing of the school year noted, "Destruction. Loss. Repair. Flourishing anew. For the Class of Andrew—still awed, still humbled, and in many cases, still shaken by the cataclysm that rocked their world—there is hope now that the circle is closing." (Brecher Article) "Green" was an end of the year theme in many schools. Other themes included rebuilding and new growth.

Just as the beginning of the school year had brought bleak futures, the close of the year brought bittersweet moments to be savored and remembered. Andrew had come in, broken their schools' windows, and seemingly sucked the school year away. What should have been the happiest of times for many seniors became the year that never really was. While the close of the school year found many students still living with relatives instead of immediate family or occupying FEMA trailers rather than permanent housing, many of these same students had found ways to overcome their tragedies and turn them into shared experiences. In this way, the shared experience of the hurricane created communalities that bonded many students with one another in ways they had never previously thought possible. For these students, unity grew out of devastation. "We're like one family, Black, Hispanic, and White. We are like brothers and sisters." (Brecher Article)

Another theme that became important was the ability to overcome adversity. There really was no other choice for many students. Some found that because their families had been victims of insurance snags, crooked contractors, or lingering unemployment, they would be graduating from high school and entering the job market instead of attending college as they had planned. In spite of these difficulties, many were planning their futures realizing that while they might have to postpone their dreams a little longer than they had wanted, they still had them. They also learned to overcome their fears. As Fred Mindermann stated, "At night, when we get a storm and its blows really hard, I start freaking bad. If you can get over this, there isn't anything you can't do." (Brecher Article) Fred's mother, Arlene, felt that it was a miracle that her son was able to finish the school year because he was so distraught about the destruction of the family home where they had lived all of Fred's life. (Brecher Article)

Michelle Burman concluded her introduction to the *Southernaire* yearbook by examining the consequences of the storm. For her, the storm brought:

> A new state of mind. . . . The storm hurt us all in incalculable ways. We lost part of ourselves . . . but we can only gain from experience. It has made us think—made us care. . . . It may seem, years from now, that we are much like we were before. But we will never forget. The results may seem small, but the efforts were . . . immeasurable. (Brecher Article)

Teachers were not as verbally optimistic or visionary. In interviewing them, *Miami Herald* reporter Brecher discovered, as we did, that the teachers were tired and worn out from the experience of rebuilding, restoring, and supporting. Rita Moore, the foreign language department chair at South Dade, explained: "You feel like you've given everything you can, and you still can't do the kind of job you really want to do. Never, ever in my life have I been so tired. I've forgotten totally how to relax." (Brecher Article) Jean Heiman, special education teacher at the same school, summarized the experience of many teachers: "I think our teachers were hit harder than our students, because not only were we trying to take care of your kids, we were trying to take care of our own kids and houses." (Brecher Article)

What are the lessons to be learned from the disaster of Hurricane Andrew? Perhaps it is still too early to recognize all of them or to identify all of the opportunities for growth provided by the experience with the storm. Perhaps we are too close to the experience to put it into an objective perspective. Yet, as we write this conclusion, nearly a year after Hurricane Andrew struck South Florida, we find ourselves asking, "What would the recovery process have been like without the schools, its teachers, and administrators?

Some lessons will only be realized as time passes. Others are still fresh in our minds. Disaster research tends to focus on the immediate consequences of an event and not on its long-term effects in shaping the lives and consciousness of a community. Events such as Hurricane Andrew and other disasters, such as the California earthquakes and the more recent Mississippi River floods, tend to fade from the national consciousness within a few weeks after media headlines turn to other emergencies and pressing topics. For those experiencing the disaster, the memory and problems remain long after the debris has been cleared and the normal living patterns have been reestablished. Memories of the event shape community perceptions and influence the community's sense of self for many years.

There is no doubt that Hurricane Andrew has been a watershed experience for South Florida. The storm represents the end of an era and the beginning of something new. Changes in housing codes and in insurance policies are only a few of the most notable modifications growing out of the rebuilding after the storm.[2] The impact of the storm and the subsequent rebuilding process have produced what could be referred to as pre- and post-Hurricane Andrew cultures, new and distinct mindsets.[3]

Watershed events are not unique in Miami's history. They are of critical importance, however, in shaping the ways that people respond to the next potential disaster or possible threat. In the case of Miami, the 1926 hurricane provided a similar turning point in the region's development. Similarly, the coming to power of Fidel Castro in January of 1959 and the subsequent exodus from Cuba over the past three decades has had an incredible impact on the ways that events are defined and responded to in the Miami area. In each case, whether the emergency was a natural disaster or the result of human events, the public schools have played a central role in adjusting to the changes imposed on the community and culture.

The role of the school in the recovery process is not typically included in traditional research in education. It is as if the school is such an important and integral part of the whole process that its presence and its role are taken for granted. What would rebuilding after Hurricane Andrew have been like if there had been no schools? What would have happened if the majority of the administrators and teachers had decided that their own personal lives and needs were so important that they had priority over teaching and rebuilding the community? What would life have been like for the Pine Villa community if their school had never had to occupy the same structure as Porter? The storm did not create the communities that we observed. It did, however, highlight the needs and problems that already existed. The aftermath of the storm also fostered strengths that might not have developed without the need to survive and rebuild. The insights that the teachers and administrators have shared with us over the past year are not typically included in traditional research on education. Nevertheless, they are critically important in interpreting outcomes and understanding why and how behaviors are shaped.

Most of the refuse and trash from the storm has been cleared away. New buildings are being constructed and old ones refurbished and restored. The financial and economic foundations of the community have been shaken and are once again being reestablished. No matter how important these aspects of the rebuilding process are, the schools did something beyond all of them. The schools provided the organizing point for bringing the community together. They provided the central themes for rebuilding. By focusing on the commonalities within the community, the schools had the power to reassure, to provide sanctuary, and to promote communication. The limitations within the individual schools also highlighted the ongoing needs of local areas and neighborhoods.

By responding quickly and effectively, the schools conveyed a strong and important message: "We are returning to normal." By providing a predictable schedule for the children and their families, the schools said, "There is continuity in our lives." By providing a place and purpose for meeting, the schools communicated, "We are here to help, to show you that we care and support your efforts." Through the efforts of the teachers, the administrators, the counselors, the secretaries, the custodians, the cafeteria workers, and the security staff, the schools helped the community cope and reestablish its own sense of direction. The schools, in effect, enabled the community to reset its own compass after the storm. None of these important acts were easy to accomplish. All of the initial rebuilding that occurred after Hurricane Andrew happened during a time of great emotional turmoil with high levels of stress and great personal discomfort for almost everyone involved. When huge areas of a metropolitan center are without electricity and water and the grocery stores and lumber yards are closed without a way to reopen, the rebuilding process becomes much more of a task than almost anyone who has not experienced such a situation can imagine. The lack of those resources to which everyone in modern day society is accustomed, the inconvenience of traveling long distances on crowded highways to obtain basic supplies that used to be available at local stores, the difficulty of trying to find carpenters, plumbers, and masons to help in rebuilding, and the anxiety associated with the lack of security caused by looters, all contributed to the overwhelming sense of frustration that most people in the impacted area experienced long after the storm was over. This period of anxiety created a time when many were happy to be at school for the simple physical comforts and companionship available there.

As important as these contributions were, it was in the psychological aspect of the reconstruction of the community that the schools have played their most important role during the year following the storm. In the bombed out neighborhoods of South Florida, the schools were the first buildings that resumed an appearance of normalcy. One of the most powerful images that comes to mind as we reflect on the events after the storm is that of driving through the unlit neighborhoods of South Kendall, passing houses with storm roofs, broken windows, and heaps of trash beyond anything we had ever imagined possible and then, seeing, off in the distance, Gilbert L. Porter Elementary School, lights shining through the darkness. Simply knowing that there the debris had been cleaned from the school yard and that there real people were going about the business of beginning the school year was an image of incredible power. Knowing that the school year really was beginning—perhaps a bit confused but nonetheless resuming the expected patterns of normal ritual and expectation—was critical for all. Life really could go on after the storm.

This opportunity to study schools in the process of rebuilding and to observe changes over time has provided us with many insights. Of all the many aspects of the rebuilding process, however, that we were able to observe, the single most important conclusion that we have gleaned is the absolute importance of the schools' role within the community and within society in general.

The study of the schools during the first year following the storm represents both a beginning and an end. The end is the completion of the initial phase of rebuilding—the reestablishment of social institutions within the community. The beginning is suggested by the realization that the study of the rebuilding process must continue. It must be viewed and revisited in the context of a larger historical time frame—one that considers and reflects on the storm and its consequences in the ongoing and evolving development of the schools themselves. This study has also made us keenly aware of the choices that American society faces in the coming years. Does our society value schools and the services provided by them? Does it support schools as it expects the schools to support the communities they serve?

POLICY RECOMMENDATIONS

Finally, in conclusion, we believe that the experience of the public schools in the aftermath of Hurricane Andrew suggests a number of approaches that are worth being considered by schools and communities facing similar disasters:

1. Crises like Hurricane Andrew should be dealt with as a problem that impacts on the entire community, not just where the main destruction occurred.

2. Local school systems should act as the central clearing house for coordinating the efforts of groups such as the Red Cross, the military, and various volunteer organizations.

3. Protocols should be established for school systems to work with agencies such as the Red Cross and the military.

4. Communication systems—i.e., cellular phone systems should be put in place under the control of school systems in order to allow restoration efforts to go on as efficiently as possible.

5. Warehouse facilities should be designated, and lists of critical supplies should be drawn up, so that when major contributions from the outside arrive maximum use can be made of them.

6. Student attendance requirements for receiving federal and state funding by schools should be temporarily suspended while the crisis is addressed.

7. Standard protocols should be set up for receiving federal and state reimbursements and should be computerized so as to speed up the payment process as much as possible.

8. Individuals, such as teachers, who provide particularly important support for children and parents in the rebuilding process, should be provided special support to help them adjust to the crisis themselves and get on with their own lives.

9. Special programs involving new curriculums or the implementation of major new procedures, should be suspended following a disaster such as Hurricane Andrew. The only exception to this should be in the case of programs such as Project Phoenix which are an immediate part of the recovery process.

NOTES

1. Brecher, Elinor J. "South Dade High Class of Andrew," *Miami Herald*, June 6, 1993, pp. 1J, 4J, 5J. The following quotes in the text are from this interview. They are cited in the text.

2. Cosgrove, John, "Remembrances of Andrew: Life Never Will Be Quite the Same," *Miami Herald*, August 24, 1993, p. 13A.

3. Proscio, Tony, "Remembrances of Andrew: Hour After Hour, Hope Lurches Away," *Miami Herald*, August 24, 1993, p. 13A.

BIBLIOGRAPHY

NEWSPAPERS

Alvarez, Lizette. "Experts: Storm Survivors Suffer Combat Symptoms." *Miami Herald*, January 9, 1993, p. 1A, 19A.

"Andrew by the Numbers." *Miami Herald*, September 24, 1992, p. 1.

Boodhoo, Niala and Alessandra Soler. "Redland Students Adjust and Wait." *Miami Herald*, Neighbors Section, April 4, 1993, pp. 1, 22.

Brecher, Elinor J. "South Dade High Class of Andrew," *Miami Herald*, June 6, 1993, pp. 1J, 4J, 5J.

Donnelly, John. "Andrew's Legacy: Kids Attempt Suicide." *Miami Herald*, March 7, 1993, pp. 1A, 12A.

Dorschner, John. "The Hurricane That Changed Everything." *Miami Herald*, August 30, 1992, pp. 1A, 30A, 31 A.

Dubocq, Tom. "South Dade Teachers Asked to Transfer to Crowded Schools." *Miami Herald*, September 23, 1992, p.1B.

————. "U.S. Promises Dade Schools All Aid Needed." *Miami Herald*, October 15, 1993, pp. 1B-4B.

————. "Storm-Displaced Students Deal with Devastated Past." *Miami Herald*, January 3, 1993, p. 1B.

Dubocq, Tom and Fran Brennan. "Stressed Out; Teachers Plead for Storm Relief." *Miami Herald*, September 25, 1992, p. 1B, 4B.

Due, Tananarive. "Air Base School Brings Back a Hint of Normalcy." *Miami Herald*, September 15, 1992, pp. 1B, 3B.

————. "Principals Share Quarters, Tough Times." *Miami Herald*, September 16, 1992, pp. 1B, 4B.

————. "School Routine Helps Teachers Avoid Self-pity." *Miami Herald*, September 17, 1992, p. 1B.

————. "Missing in Action: Students Wonder Where Friends Have Gone. *Miami Herald*, September 18, 1992, pp. 1B, 2B.

————. "Laughter, Fears Draw First Week to a Close." *Miami Herald*, September 19, 1992, pp. 1B, 4B.

———— . "Air Base Elementary Revisited." *Miami Herald*, December 14, 1992, pp. 1C, 2C.

Epstein, Gail. "After Andrew Many Kids are Talking, Drawing—Coping." *Miami Herald*, September 18, 1992, pp. 1E, 3E.

Fiedler, Tom. "Storm Drives Home the Need for Leadership." *Miami Herald*, August 30, 1992, p. 4L.

Getter, Lisa. "Loss of 15 Homes Unites Family of 65." *Miami Herald*, August 27, 1992, pp. 1, 2B.

Goldstein, Laurie. "School Routine Soothes Andrew's Trauma." *Washington Post*, September 16, 1992, p. A4.

Kleinberg, Howard. "Support Restoration of Historic Redland School." *Miami Herald*, April 13, 1993, p. 7A.

Marks, Marilyn. "Dade Teenagers Yearn for Return to Their Own Schools, Old Friends." *Miami Herald*, September 15, 1992, p. 3B.

Martin, Lydia. "Seabees Help Schools Get Shipshape Again." *Miami Herald*, September 8, 1992, p. 1B.

"Measuring a Hurricane's Strength." *Miami Herald*, August 28, 1992, p. 3E.

Monroe, Linda. "Helping Your Children Cope." *Miami Herald*, September 4, 1992, pp. 1E, 2E, 3E.

Morgan, Curtis and Stephen K. Doig. "Could It Happen Again?" *Miami Herald*, September 5, 1992, pp. 1E, 7E.

O'Neill, Jon. "Dade Schools Facing 2-week Delay." *Miami Herald*, August 27, 1992, pp. 1A, 16A.

———— . "South Dade Schools Face Major Repairs." *Miami Herald*, August 30, 1992, p. 18C.

———— . "Perrine Elementary on Rebound." *Miami Herald*, October 11, 1992, p. 19B.

———— . "School Construction in a Jumble." *Miami Herald*, October 20, 1992, pp. 1b and 3b.

———— . "Caribbean Elementary: Long Road to Repair." *Miami Herald*, Neighbors Section, January 3, 1992, p. 18.

———— . "For Music Teacher, Job is Best Way to Hit High Notes." *Miami Herald*, Neighbors Section, January 31, 1993, p. 26.

————. "Silver Lining: Hurricane Experience Forges Bond at School." *Miami Herald*, Neighbors Section, February 11, 1993, pp. 1, 18, 20.

O'Neill, Jon and Marcia Smith. "School's In for Seekers of Shelter." *Miami Herald*, September 2, 1992, p. 13A.

O'Neill, Jon, Ana Acle, and Patrick May. "Dade Schools Bracing for the First Day." *Miami Herald*, September 10, 1992, p. 1B.

Parks, Arva Moore. "Until Last Week, Storm of '26 Was *the* Hurricane." *Miami Herald*, August 30, 1992, pp. 1L, 5L.

Pravia, Cristina I., "Pine Villa Needs Help Parents Say." *Miami Herald*, Neighbors Section, December 6, 1992, p. 38.

Pravia, Cristina I. and Jon O'Neill. "Split Decisions: Students, Teachers Make Best of Staggered Schedules." *Miami Herald*, Neighbors Section, January 10, 1993, pp. 18, 19.

Proscio, Tony. "What Do We Say to Our Children?" *Miami Herald*, September 8, 1992, p. 21a.

Satterfield, David. "Pulling Up Stakes: Thousands Planning to Relocate Because of Andrew." *Miami Herald*, November 10, 1992, p. 1A.

Soler, Alessandra. "Learning to Share a School." *Miami Herald*, Neighbors Section, May 13, 1993, pp. 18-19.

Steinberg, Glenn R. "Teacher, Pine Villa Elementary School." *Miami Herald*, September 19, 1992, p. 22A.

Strouse, Charles and Rachel Swarns. "Back to school: Dade Races to Make Repairs." *Miami Herald*, September 14, 1992, pp. 1, 12a.

"Teachers seek delay in programs." *Miami Herald*," March 5, 1993, p. 2B.

Wolin, John. "After Storm of Lifetime—A Rebirth." *Miami Herald*, May 23, 1993, p. 1G, 7G.

OTHER SOURCES

Dade County Public Schools. *District and School Profiles, 1991-1992*. Miami: Dade County Public Schools, 1992.

————. *Hurricane Andrew Recovery Plan*. Miami: Dade County Public Schools, 1992.

Diegmueller, Karen and Mark Pitsch. "Hurricane Deals Harsh Blow to Fla., La. Schools," *Education Week* 12, no. 1 (September 9, 1992): pp. 1, 22-23.

Geipel, Robert. *Long-Term Consequences of Disasters: The Reconstruction of Friuli, Italy, and its International Context, 1976-1988.* New York: Springer-Verlag, 1991.

Geis, Tarja and Frederic Zerlin. *Saturn School Project*, October 27, 1989, internal school document.

Kleinberg, Howard. *The Florida Hurricane and Disaster, 1992.* Miami: Centennial Press, 1992.

Miami Herald (members of the staff). *The Big One.* Kansas City, MO: Andrews and McMeel, 1992.

Pitsch, Mark. "Down But Not Out, Patched Dade Schools Open." *Education Week* 12, no. 3 (September 1992): pp. 1, 14, 15.

Reardon, L. F. *The Florida Hurricane and Disaster.* Miami: Centennial Press, 1992. Reprint of the 1926 edition of Reardon's *The Florida Hurricane and Disaster.*

Rist, Marilee C. "Miami's Iron Man." *The Executive Educator* (March 1993): pp. 29-32.

Smith, Louis M. and William Geoffrey. *The Complexities of an Urban Classroom: An Analysis Toward a General Theory of Teaching.* New York: Holt, Rinehart and Winston, 1968.

Sun-Sentinel, Andrew! Savagery From the Sea, August 24, 1992. Orlando, Florida: Tribune Publishing, 1992.

Visiedo, Octavio. "Status Report #1: 1992 Opening of Schools/Hurricane Andrew," Internal Memorandum, Dade County Public Schools, September 15, 1992.

————. "Status Report #2: 1992 Opening of Schools/Hurricane Andrew," Internal Memorandum, Dade County Public Schools, September 17, 1992.

————. "Status Report #3: 1992 Opening of Schools/Hurricane Andrew," Internal Memorandum, Dade County Public Schools, September 21, 1992.

————. "Status Report #4: 1992 Opening of Schools/Hurricane Andrew," Internal Memorandum, Dade County Public Schools, October 5, 1992.

INDEX